Underrated Rock Book

The 200 Most Overlooked Albums
1970-2015

Jim Santora Jr

Underrated Rock Book is dedicated to the memory of Ron Roff

Acknowledgments

A few people that were instrumental in offering many suggestions as a part of my research: thanks to Dominick Schork, Jim Mosley, Wayne Gonzalez, Jeff Morin, Byron Crowley, Chris Dymmel, Jordan Borenstein, Kevin Law, John Erickson, Dan Chrzan, Rob Mallory, and Steve Shaver. Thanks to all of the radio programs, stations and music pages that helped me get the word out about this project: Raven Radio & Rock City Demolition, Philly Rock Radio & The Saloon Rock Club Radio Show, Andy Julia, Larry Errera & The Idiots Radio Show, Lisa Cook (Tainted's Music Pit) and Musical WTH. Special thanks go to all the people over the years that I have had the opportunity to work with where music was involved. All the writing jobs, DJ gigs, radio station stints and various bands that I got to perform, record and rock people's faces off. Each one of these opportunities put me on the path to continue to explore music and encourage me to finally sit down and put my thoughts on paper: John Weissner (aka JT Rage), Ed Mason, Jason Mento, Kurt Dillon, Paul Pernice, Don Valentino, Rick Drill, Leroy Hickman, Jonathan "Dizzle" Davis, Michael "Angel" Cruz, Rich Petkevis, Scott Quinn, Lex Santana & Hot Rock Radio, Chris Leone, Greg Orlandini, Chuck Penza, Jimmy Caputo, Steve Cavico, Nate Zilla, Winnie Winters-Craft, Chris "Bundy" Howe Steve Nakovich and my brother John Santora. A huge thank you to all the artists, management, record labels and public relation companies that took time to respond to e-mails and submitting photos for the book. It is very appreciative to all of you. Special thanks to Catherine Jean Hubbard, Chip Ruggeri, Steve Karas, Eric Alper, Alan Moy, Michael Pilmer, Deb Klein, Corrosion of Conformity, Steve Blaze of Lillian Axe, Ruthie Morris of Magnapop, Devi Akanand, Peter Wark, Randy Jackson of Zebra, Beth Fieger Falkenstein, Chris Penn from Tripping Daisy, BC from Weaving the Fate, Chris Adam from Smash Into

Pieces, Ron Burman from Mascot Records, Sean Danielson of Smile Empty Soul, Louie St. August of Mass, Sallie McManus, Ben Owen, Mermaid Records, Robert Toren, Jeremy Johnson of Core, Rebeca Qualls of Recovery Council and Darrell Millar of Killer Dwarfs. To my parents, Linda, and James Santora Sr: Thanks for allowing me to rock, even though it was too loud, and you didn't understand all of it. For letting me rummage through the family entertainment center to listen to all the 45's, Albums and 8-Tracks as a kid. That collection was a great starting place. Thanks to my children Joshua and Abbie: As the two of you got more into music, you both seem to have gotten some of your musical genes from your Dad. Which I have seen in some of the direction music has taken both of you. Some of the selections for this book have been directly or indirectly the result of music you managed to bring to my airwaves over the years. Love you both. My final thanks go to my wife Jennifer: Thank you for giving me the opportunity to sit down and finally write this book. You have also influenced me as well. Your tastes are different from mine, and that gave me a chance to listen to some of your favorite artists, which were intriguing and opened plenty of other directions for how this book took shape. Words do not express how much I appreciate you. Love you always and forever.

Table of Contents

Are You Ready To Rock? An Introduction

Underrated comes from the word Underrate. A verb meaning underestimates the extent, value, or importance (of someone or something). Being underrated or considered that is really a matter of opinion and always open to debate. Examples from sports, movies, hobbies and even what we do at our place of work could be considered underrated, though the same argument could be said about being overrated as well.

The Underrated Rock Book was the culmination of my lifelong fascination and love of music. I have always had this idea of capturing some of the most underappreciated and overlooked artists and albums in one forum. My introduction to rock music began by raiding my parent's music collection back in the early 1970's. Where Elvis, Beach Boys, Elton John, and Chicago among others became my starting point. My Aunt gave me a copy of the Kiss "Destroyer" album for Christmas in 1976. From that point on, I got into heavier rock music. In addition to Kiss, my favorite bands going into my teenage years were Cheap Trick, Rush, and Aerosmith. As I started high school, I was into hard rock and heavy metal, but I was a closet new waver and used to hide my Simple Mind 45's behind my Judas Priest albums. By the time I graduated, my collection of favorites had included artists like The Cult, Dokken, and Loudness.

Graduating high school, I really had no plan. I didn't know what I wanted to do. As a kid, I used to play Disc Jockey in my room but never thought of it as a career choice. That was until I enrolled at Atlantic Community College and found out there was an in-house radio station. It was called WACC (or Radio WACC, pronounced wack), and it was a free-form station. This was my home for the next three years. During my time, I really got into so many styles of rock music, I was blown away by how many artists I had not listened to. I would do a metal show, an alternative rock show and then some hodgepodge shows of anything I could get my hands on. One of the cool things during this time was that I got to listen to all the cool 90's bands when they weren't cool yet. Soundgarden, Nirvana, Red Hot Chili Peppers, Soul Asylum, Goo Goo Dolls are a few that come off the top of my head. Pearl Jam was Mother Love Bone, and Cracker was Camper Van Beethoven.

As the years have gone on, I have written for various music magazines and had my own radio programs. One of the things I have enjoyed over these years is all the music I have had the opportunity to listen to. I also became be a singer in some rock bands and by doing so, had a much deeper appreciation for so many of the artists that have been overlooked in their time. Because at one time early on for the most successful artists, they were once cast-offs, underappreciated and unknown to the masses.

So how do we come up with what is in the Underrated Rock Book? First, we set up some guidelines. Because if I didn't put anything in place, we would see 5 albums from Cheap Trick, every album from King's X and that would not be much fun to read (or maybe it would, an idea for next time). Below are the guidelines used to create our list of 200 Most Underrated Rock Albums:

Albums must fall into the "rock" genre' (Trust me, you're reading this, and yes, it's going to be all over the place)
Albums must be between the years 1970-2015 (I was born in 1969, so I needed a starting point)
Only one album per artist (So you will not see a repeat from the same band/artist). However….
Bands/Artists that have solo albums or other groups they were a part of are eligible for the list. (There are some crossovers and solo releases)

No Live Albums or Greatest Hits releases are allowed on the list

Easy enough, but we did get suggestions from people that were a part of the book's Facebook page. We also had feedback from various DJ's and musicians I have been associated with over the years. This feedback was critical to the collection of music that was put together.

Is this book perfect? No. Will you disagree with this book? Probably, and I hope you do. This book is to be used as a guide to perhaps go back and listen to artists you are not familiar with. Or that artist you hated 20 years ago. Time for a second spin? Debate with your friends and compare notes. It's a book that I put together to have as a discussion piece. So be sure to be near your computer or any music device where you can get a chance to listen to artists and various tracks as you read. That's part of the point of this book. It has an option to multitask. Pick up the book and as soon as there is something that interests you, dial-up YouTube or Spotify (or talk to Alexa) and give it a listen. Because unless you're marking down artists you want to check out, you might forget, put down the book and once again, that album is overlooked.

So, get ready to crank it up as you are going to be taken onto a musical journey full of bands you are going to remember or wonder why this is the first time you have ever heard them before. Welcome to the Underrated Rock Book.

0-A

7 Seconds – The Music, The Message (Sony/BMI - 1995) Punk

In the mid-90s, there was a punk rock revolution. Well, not in the traditional sense. As bands like Green Day and The Offspring made their mark on MTV and in the process, sold millions of albums, it was time to snatch up all the punk bands from the past and sign them to major labels. Meaning bands that had carved out a niche in the 80s like 7 Seconds entered the world of the majors in 1995 with *The Music, The Message*. While the songs on this release have more of a gloss pop-punk production style, the band continues to create melodic, fast-paced punk rock songs. Despite the call-up to the majors, 7 Seconds failed to get much out of radio airplay for this release, meaning songs like "See You Tomorrow," "Punk Rock Teeth" and the title track missed a lot of ears along the way. 7 Seconds would leave the majors as quickly as they got there and have continued to release material and tour over the years to an underground following.

54.40 – Show Me (Warner - 1987) Alternative Rock

A popular band in their home country of Canada, yet unknown to most people in the US. 54.40 was an alternative rock band that put together some solid, lighthearted rock. If they had some ears outside of the Great

White North, they had the tools to make it as a favorite group in the states. In 1987, the band released *Show Me*, which basically became known in some college radio airplay charts and that's where it ends. Tracks like "One Day In Your Life," the rockier "Walk In Line" and "One Gun" showcase a band that at the time could have been a Canadian version of R.E.M. Similarities are there but 54.40 is clearly its own band with their own vision. Despite the band's lack of success outside of Canada, they did score a hit with the song "I Go Blind" when Hootie & The Blowfish covered it in 1995. 54.40 continues rocking primarily in Canada today proudly staying together now for 35+ years.

54.40 (photo by Elizabeth Zeschin)

77 – Maximum Rock N Roll (Listenable - 2013) Hard Rock

AC/DC may be one of the most recognizable and influential bands of their time. While there are plenty of groups that try to get that style, sound, and vocals of Bon Scott or Brian Johnson. The only artist that comes close is

Spain's 77. In 2013, they would release *Maximum Rock N Roll*, and if there was a blind listening test, you would think you were listening to some 70s unreleased tracks from Angus and the boys. This is three-chord rock n roll at its finest. This album was primarily released in Europe, and unless you are searching, you pretty much missed this disc. Standout tracks include the power stomp of "Down And Dirty," the pro-alcohol track "Stay Away From Water" and "Don't You Scream." These tracks and others show a band that read the AC/DC bible line for line. Truly a standout album track for track and if you are a fan of AC/DC, this is a great listen for a band that really hasn't had much push in the U.S. 77 may be one of the best-kept secrets in hard rock.

1978 Champs – Ansiah (Infamous Empire - 2013) Indie Rock

A band with a combination of Punk, Emo, and Southern Rock sounds, 1978 Champs brought a unique and fresh sound out when releasing *Ansiah* in 2013. This Atlanta band had something that you couldn't put the finger on after one listen. This is one album where you need to listen to it multiple times to truly understand where they were coming from. The standout track is "Alamo." This track is the perfect combination of what modern/alternative rock and southern rock sound like, further proving that the band has studied their southern and Atlanta roots. Other songs weave between the boundaries of acoustic/folk stylings and the southern rock we previously mentioned. Some other highlights include the emo-folk of "Pals" and the rocker "200 Years". This was a band that shortly disbanded, which is unfortunate for most people that did not get a chance to hear them. If you are fans of emo style rock and southern rock, this is a must listen.

AC/DC – Fly On The Wall (Atlantic - 1986) Hard Rock

Let's face facts. AC/DC is probably one of the greatest bands in music period. One can take their discography and put it up against all the greats. We also can't forget that *Back In Black* is one of the greatest selling albums of all time. Which then brings us to 1986 and *Fly On The Wall*. After the success of *Back In Black*, they followed with *For Those About to Rock* and *Dirty Deeds Done Dirt Cheap* (which was from the Bon Scott days never issued in the U.S.). AC/DC was at the highest point of their career. Then they dropped *Flick Of The Switch*. I can tell you that I can't even name a song from that release. It's like Angus, Brian and the gang had the rug pulled out from under them. So, the follow-up was *Fly on The Wall*. The band does what they do best. Straight up hard rock with no frills and probably the best group to do more with less. Songs like "Shake Your Foundations," "Sink The Pink" and "Hell Or High Water" should have been radio staples at the time. However, the band continued to slide on the charts as *Fly On The Wall* only made it to #32. In the AC/DC collection, this album is the hidden gem.

Aerosmith – Night In The Ruts (Columbia-1979) Hard Rock

It was 1976 when Aerosmith was at their peak. With the release of Rocks, this was a band that couldn't be stopped. Along with Kiss, they were probably two of the most prominent groups of that time. However, it was also the beginning of a downward spiral for the band from Boston. They would release *Draw The Line*, which failed to match up to Rocks. Then they were the "villain" band in the *Sgt. Pepper's Lonely Hearts Club Band* movie (the movie which would kill Peter Frampton's career). When it came time to begin recording *Night In The Ruts*, drugs and alcohol were taking a toll on the band, not to mention some friction amongst the members. Things got so bad, that guitarist Joe Perry quit the band, forcing Aerosmith to bring in two other guitarists to finish his parts. When it's all said and done, this became a bargain bin release. However, one needs to give another listen to what's an amazing record. The opening tracks "No Surprise" and "Chiquita" are classic Aerosmith. Followed by "Remember (Walking In The Sand)," a re-make made famous by the Shangri-Las. Steven Tyler and company, despite all the issues surrounding the band, continued to chug along as the blues side of the band was front and center on "Cheese Cake", which is one of the standouts on this release, along with the jam rocker "Three Mile Smile" and the heavy cover of The Yardbirds "Think About It". The album closes with a ballad "Mia," which shows Tyler's amazing vocal work. It's surprising that this was not a hit on the radio like "Dream On'. Sadly, this train would come off the tracks, and guitarist Brad Whitford would follow Perry out of the band. They would return in 1985 and become one of the biggest comeback stories in rock history En-route to a Hall of Fame-worthy career. Perhaps that doesn't happen if *Night In The Ruts* doesn't end up in the bargain bin?

Alice In Chains – Sap (Sony - 1992) Hard Rock

When Alice In Chains came onto the rock/metal scene in 1990, they were already making waves. There were a host of new bands bringing in new sounds in what was soon to become an overblown glam metal scene. *Facelift* was a huge success thanks to songs like "Man In The Box" and in 1992, they changed the rules and released *Sap*, a four-song EP of acoustic songs. This only added to the mystique of the type of band Alice In Chains was, showing the melodic side of the band as well as showing that this band could slug out metal riffs as well as the ability to strip it back. The EP also features Heart's Ann Wilson and Soundgarden's Chris Cornell, only adding to the highlights of this disc. Songs like "Got Me Wrong," "Right Turn" and "Brother" all could have been huge songs on a full-length album. *Sap* managed to go gold and Dirt was released later in 1992 and proved to be even more successful than *Facelift*. Alice In Chains has produced some great songs in the Layne Staley era. In that mix, there is a hidden gem of an EP that needs to be included in that discussion.

The Angels – Beyond Salvation (Chrysalis - 1990) Hard Rock

For those not familiar with The Angels, they are a hard-rocking Australian band that got their start in 1977 and influenced bands like Guns N Roses, Nirvana and Pearl Jam. They would release *Beyond Salvation*, which would be a #1 smash in their home country, but could they reach that feat in the US? Their sound was a combination of straight-up rock, some fellow countrymate AC/DC stomp and at times, ZZ Top. Highlights of this album are the Tex-Mex synth boogie of "Back Street Pick Up," the groove of "Dogs Are Talking" and the blues sounds of "Pushing and Shoving." It's a great soundscape of rock from front to back. However, *Beyond Salvation* does not put a significant dent in the American rock scene. They were inducted into the ARIA Hall of Fame in 1998 and posted six top ten albums in their home country. This may be a band you never heard of and should know today. *Beyond Salvation* deserves your attention.

Ancient VVisdom – Sacrificial (Magic Bullet - 2014) Occult Rock

Of course, most people have no idea what Occult Rock or Death Rock is. Others feel it's bands like Ghost, which is true, but you need to go deeper. When I first heard Ancient VVisdom (not a misprint, it's Wisdom with two V's), I was hooked. When *Sacrificial* was released, the sound was perfect. This music is the soundtrack to hell. Forget everything you think about hell. It is not Slayer or death metal. On *Sacrificial*, the music and vocals are melodic. Not to mention that the band has no problems adding acoustic guitars into the mix. Some of the songs that are Satan's favorites include "The Devil's Work," "Chaos Will Reign" and "Blind Leading The Blind."

Lyrically, Ancient VVisdom is a breath of fresh air to any other artists you listen too. You will find no love songs, no sex, drugs and so on. Just death, Satan, and sacrifices. Of course, this style of music is not what parents and other civilized people want you to listen to. Which probably explains why they are an indie band. There is no confusing the talent or originality of this band. A must-listen but not for the weak.

...And You Will Know Us By The Trail Of Dead – Worlds Apart (Interscope - 2005) Alternative Rock

A band that makes it mark in alternative rock but could also be classified as noise and progressive rock as well, Trail Of Dead are an interesting band. Primarily a band comprised of two members who are multi-instrumentalists and able to bring in various other players into their brand of organized musical chaos. On *Worlds Apart*, the band covers a lot of different territories, and it is hard to classify the band. They do have the experimental rock part down, and the more you listen, you are wondering what they will do next. It's not always polished, but it's not supposed to be. Then they will belt out a chorus that sounds like everyone is singing in a local drinking establishment like heard on the title track, which then ends with various animal sound effects? Is this just strange or genius? The band shows a pure progressive rock focus on "A Classic Art Showcase" with an indie rock flair. While "Will You Smile Again For Me" is a blistering six-minute Alterna-prog classic that most people have never had the opportunity to hear. Trail Of Dead is not afraid to use any instruments that can be provided to them and it shows on this release. *Worlds Apart* is their highest charting album. With some more opportunities outside of college radio, there may have been more intrigued listeners looking for a band to amaze them both musically and sonically, could have given them more exposure. Maybe it's another band with a strange name or is it that the music is so over the heads of the general listener?

Angel – S/T (Casablanca - 1975) Progressive Rock

Angel was a prog rock/hard rock band that was discovered by Gene Simmons of Kiss, and that led to the group having their debut album on the same Casablanca label. The album is full of synthesizers/keyboards by Greg Giuffria, which really stand out in the band's sound. Vocalist Frank DiMino has a very dynamic range and has some similarities to Robert Plant in some songs. One of the massive standout tracks is the opening track "Tower," led by its space-age battle synths and angelic beginning to the song, followed by some well thought out song structures. Other standout tracks include "Long Time" and the heavier "Broken Dreams." Angel has more of a cult following and never gathered the audience they craved. As their career moved through the 70s, the band shifted away from the prog rock sounds into more of a hard rock/glam rock sound. While they continued to develop as a band, their debut is the best of the bunch, and we can all wonder if breaking away from the prog rock was a good idea.

Anthrax – Stomp 442 (Elektra - 1995) Heavy Metal

If you are a fan of Thrash Metal, then you know that Anthrax, along with Metallica, Slayer and Megadeth are the "Big 4" of the genre and pretty much every other band that followed had to live up to these artists. As the 80s would fade, these bands would shift gears in the 90s with grunge and alternative metal taking over the landscape. Anthrax would make a huge switch adding vocalist John Bush from Armored Saint to replace Joey Belladonna, who had served the band well with his vocal talents. The first album with Bush proved to be a Top 10 hit with *Sound Of White Noise*. Album #2 with Bush shows the band firing on all cylinders with the track "Fueled." Other songs like the acoustic-led "Bare" and "Nothing" show the various range the band was doing at the time. *Stomp 442* did not get the same pop from fans at the time, perhaps not in favor of the band's direction. It is the first of their albums that did not go gold after a four-album run of doing so. After 20+ years, this album needs a re-listen to show that despite the changes in direction, Anthrax was one of the few bands that could pull it off.

April Wine – Harder… Faster (Capitol - 1979) Hard Rock

I am pretty sure for most people if you ask them about April Wine, they will tell you they sing "Just Between You And Me" but that's if people even remember this band. This Canadian band has been around since 1969, and yes in 1981, they became huge with the previously mentioned song from the classic *Nature Of The Beast*. In 1979, April Wine would release *Harder… Faster*, which would become a gold-selling album for the band in the US (They were already huge in Canada). The band's central focus was on vocal harmonies and at times, three guitarists. Nothing shows off that three guitar-sound than the opening track "I Like To Rock." The best part of the song is when they get to the end, and you hear guitar parts for the main track, "Day Tripper" from the Beatles and "Satisfaction" from the Rolling Stones in one ultimate mashup. Other tracks like the rocker "Ladies Man" and the melodic "Before The Dawn" show that April Wine was just getting started and hadn't even reached their full potential. Success would come shortly after and then the band slid out of the spotlight. Outside of "I Like To Rock" getting an occasional spin on Classic Rock radio, *Harder… Faster* is an overlooked classic.

The Atomic Bitchwax – 3 (Meteor City - 2005) Stoner Rock

While many genres get overlooked, Stoner Rock/Metal has a special place in the underrated ranks. Many of the bands in the genre are usually multi classified in the process. The Atomic Bitchwax is one of those artists. On their third release, simply titled *3,* they are a cross of Danko Jones meets

Monster Magnet, with some psychedelic and progressive textures thrown in. It's a surprise how a cool speedy rocker like "The Destroyer" doesn't crack rock radio airwaves. Other songs deserving some attention is the guitar-driven "You Oughta Know," which has a bluesy feel and the prog textures of "Maybe I'm A Leo," which also contains some melodic chorus harmonies. The Atomic Bitchwax is still releasing new music and hasn't changed their style. You don't fix what isn't broken, and since 1999, they have been an overlooked secret outside of some stoner circles.

Audiovent – Dirty Sexy Knights In Paris (Atlantic - 2002) Hard Rock

Audiovent could also be called Incubus Jr as both vocalist Jason Boyd and guitarist Benjamin Einziger are brothers of Brandon Boyd and Mike Einziger respectfully. While listening to *Dirty Sexy Knights In Paris* will be sure to draw comparisons between the two bands, Audiovent is clearly more straight-up rock than Incubus. Jason Boyd had a fantastic voice and showcased throughout this album. With tracks like the powerful "The Energy," the more acoustic/electric melodic driven "One Small Choice" and "Stalker," which could have ended up on an Incubus record. Perhaps that was the problem with Audiovent. For as much talent that they had and putting out a great album, they could not get out of the shadow of their brothers. Audiovent would not release another album as creative-differences would split the band up.

B-C

The Bags – Rock Starve (Restless - 1987) Alternative Rock

One band with an infectious sound but under the radar was the three-piece band from New England known as The Bags. Not to be confused with the punk band from the 70s, this band was some sort of a cross breed of The Ramones, Kiss, Motorhead, The Who and any other punk, hard rock and classic rock bands you can mention. In 1987, they would release *Rock Starve*, and it does not disappoint. From the opening jammer "Spread It Around," The Who tinged "What Do You Want" and the bottom end heaviness of "Nothing To Say To You" that makes you wonder if it's a lost Kiss track. The album sways into a lower end heavy/punk speed vibe throughout. We could also wonder if the Kurt Cobain's of the world and Seattle, in general, were listening to The Bags alongside their Dinosaur Jr. and Husker Du albums. Sadly, The Bags were a severely overlooked band that have continued to release records over the years. *Rock Starve* is going to be a hard find as it is not available outside of paying $100-$200 on various internet sites.

Bad Brains – Quickness (Caroline - 1989) Hardcore

Bad Brains are not just hardcore punk, they are actual pioneers of the genre that have paved the way for just about everyone after them. As part of the DC Hardcore scene, they even got a Rock N Roll Hall of Fame nod in 2016, which should say something about a band that never scored much success on the charts or mainstream radio. *Quickness* was released in 1989, and the follow up to 1986's *I Against I*, which has been listed in several polls as one of the must listen to albums of all time. On *Quickness*, Bad

Brains combine their hardcore punk with metal, reggae, funk, and hip-hop and genuinely are an original band. From the opening number "Soul Craft" which carries a funk metal tone, "Silent Tears" and "Voyage To Infinity" which shows the band going more into the metal realm. In the meantime, the group stays true to their roots with this release, and if you are listening to Bad Brains for the first time, this should be an album in the mix.

Bad Religion – The Grey Race (Atlantic - 1996) Punk Rock

Bad Religion got its start back in 1979 and have influenced bands like The Offspring, AFI and Rise Against in their 30+ year career. During the 90s, Bad Religion got their break, and in 1994 they would release *Stranger Than Fiction* and reach gold status. The thought was the next release (at the time their 9th album) would take them to the next level. In 1996, they would release *The Grey Race*. While most of the punk bands of the time were more radio-friendly (Green Day, The Offspring), Bad Religion was straight up punk rock. They never stopped having the edge that made them so influential. While the album had some great songs like the catchy "A Walk," the quickness of "Nobody Listens" and the lyrical and political message of "The Streets Of America," it was missing something that the newer bands had for radio and MTV. Meaning that Bad Religion stayed more of a second-tier punk band in the 90s when they should have been much more significant. Good news is that Bad Religion has continued to release great albums staying true to their roots and do not show any signs of slowing down.

Badlands – S/T (Atlantic - 1989) Hard Rock

Some would say this is a supergroup of sorts that put together one of the most underrated albums of the 80s. The band was comprised of Jake E. Lee, who was the guitarist for Ozzy Osbourne, Ray Gillen (vocals) and Eric Singer (drums), who were in Black Sabbath together (Singer with Kiss afterward) and bassist Greg Chaisson. Musically, the Badlands debut is stellar. Featuring the incredible six-string work of Lee and the fantastic vocals of Gillen. This should have been an album that topped the charts in 1989. With solid tracks like "Dreams In The Dark," "Winter's Call" and "High Wire," it is really one of those head scratchers as to why it did not. Overall, the album had a great blues hard rock feel throughout, with moments of southern rock thrown in. Gillen's vocals soar throughout and show just how underappreciated he was as a vocalist. Tensions with the band derailed Badlands before they really got it going. They would eventually break up, not really making any noise with their follow up release *Voodoo Highway*. The death of Gillian in 1993 would pretty much end any idea of Badlands reforming.

Balaam and the Angel – Live Free Or Die (Virgin - 1988) Rock

A band of brothers from the UK with roots in the goth rock genre, Baalam, and the Angel toured with The Cult. Being that Ian, Billy, and company were morphing from their goth/new wave sound for something more AC/DC at the time, Balaam and the Angel would shift towards more of a hard rock edge with *Live Free Or Die*. The results are what should have been a pure rock classic. The lead track "I'll Show You Something Special" is a road style rocker that found its way in the Steve Martin/John Candy movie *Planes, Trains, and Automobiles*. Meanwhile, "I Love The Things You Do To Me" was a catchy melodic rocker which should have been a heavy radio staple. Other songs like the title track and "Long Time Loving You" continue with the catchy melodies and powerful rock stomp. However, the timing might have been the issue with Balaam and the Angel. Their sound-change happened before The Cult's next transformation in 1989 with Sonic Temple, which was a Top 10 album. Perhaps a release after that album would have been more of a successful outcome for this now hidden rocker.

Beastie Boys – Check Your Head (Capitol - 1992) Alternative Rock

While the Beastie Boys will always be remembered for "Fight For Your Right" and "Sabotage," most fans do not realize that the band was part of the early hardcore NYC punk scene of the 1980's. The element of hip-hop was in full effect at the time, and the Beastie Boys embraced it. Enough to get the attention of Rick Rubin and the rest was history. After 1986's *License To Ill*, the band took a step back with 1989's *Paul's Boutique*. When *Check Your Head* was released in 1992, the band went back to playing instruments and incorporating some of their hardcore roots into their music. *Check Your Head* has a dark, lo-fi sound and would pave their way into the 90s. With tracks like "So What'Cha Want," "Jimmy James" and the punk rock attitude of "Gratitude," Ad-Roc, Mike D and MCA put together a real rock/hip-hop masterpiece. This album breaks the mold of what rock and hip-hop were previously, where it was more pop radio then rock radio (Rage Against The Machine was also coming into play in 1992 as well). I would also say that there were a few artists from the Nu Metal 90s that were cranking up *Check Your Head* as an influence.

Billy Squier – Hear and Now (Capitol - 1989) Rock

In the early 1980s, Billy Squier pretty much came out of nowhere and songs like "The Stroke," "Everybody Wants You" and "Lonely Is the Night" still rock radio staples today. However, in the mid-80s it all started to go south. Many place fault on the MTV video for "Rock Me Tonight."

Others could credit the height of the glam bands as well. Let's face it, Billy Squier had been around since the early 70s performing with the band Piper and even touring with Kiss before his solo career started in 1980. Squier was a great songwriter, and his songs were perfect for rock radio at the time. In fact, he even was enough hard rock to get that fan base as well. With his career on the downslope, he released *Hear And Now* in 1989 which seem to provide some life. There was a new energy in these songs probably not heard since his earlier recordings. He managed to carve out another radio hit with "Don't Say You Love Me," while the opening track "Rock Out/Punch Somebody" had some thump and groove. The best track from the album is the ballad "Don't Let Me Go." This was a song that perhaps on his earlier records, would have been a huge hit. It proved to be short-lived single and should get a second listen for people that missed it the first time. Billy Squier's overall collection is full of great songs and Hear and Now is clearly an overlooked album that deserves another spin to see just how much of a great artist he was.

Blue Oyster Cult – The Revolution By Night (Columbia - 1983) Classic Rock

The case of Blue Oyster Cult is fascinating. The band's roots go back to the late 60s and always a head-scratcher in-regards to what kind of group they were. They were a band that could blend psychedelic, prog, and hard rock and make nothing into something, not always to ultimate success. That changed in 1976 with the release of "Don't Fear (The Reaper)." Suddenly the band was huge and continued a successful run which would continue into the early 80s. By 1983, B.O.C. was going more into a melodic hard rock sound which was staying in the direction their sound was headed. *The Revolution By Night* should have continued their successful run. However, this is where everything stops. One would need to question why when songs like the harder rocker "Take Me Away" was in the vein of 1981 hit

"Burnin For You." Other songs like the somber "Shooting Shark" (complete with its 80s feel of melodic textures, throbbing bass lines, and heavy synths) and "Eyes Of Fire" should have all been much bigger songs for the band. However, it would appear the band dove right into the 80s sound style and embraced it, while fans of the band probably hoped they would hear more "Godzilla" type rockers. *The Revolution By Night* is the beginning of the slide for B.O.C., but it shouldn't have been and has been a scapegoat for the band's downfall.

Donald "Buck" Dharma of Blue Oyster Cult (photo by Byron Crowley)

Blues Traveler – Straight On Till Morning (A&M - 1997) Rock

Blues Traveler was already a successful blues-rock band before 1994's *Four* took them to new heights, selling 6 million copies thanks to songs like "Run Around" and "Hook." In 1997, John Popper and company released *Straight On Till Morning* and even though it went platinum, it is clearly an overlooked album. Starting with the first track "Carolina Blues," which is flat out one awesome blues song. Let's also point out that Popper is one of the best harmonica players on the planet and lets everything hang out on the track. Other songs like "Most Precarious" and "Last Night I Dreamed" show a band that bleeds the blues. Like many artists, it's sometimes hard to duplicate mega-success, and that seems to be the fate of *Straight On Till Morning*, which is an album that deserves a re-listen.

Boston – Third Stage (MCA - 1986) Classic Rock

This will be one album that I am sure will cause some discussion as to why is it on the list. As I write this, I have my own doubts, then I took a check over on Spotify and wanted to see how Boston songs fair. A look at their Top 10 revealed 8 songs from their debut. From *Third Stage* only "Amanda" cracked the list. Of course, this album went through a lot of turmoil to get to its eventual release in 1986. First, it took eight years between releases thanks to some legal battles. By the time everything is said and done, the only members left from the first two albums are master-mind guitarist/producer Tom Sholtz and vocalist Brad Delp. *Third Stage* stands up with any of the 70s albums. With songs like "We're Ready," "Cool The Engines" and another "Amanda" style power ballad with "Hollyann." It was an album that went 4 times platinum, but 30 years later, it doesn't seem to get the love the debut or even *Don't Look Back* received. I am sure there are a few collections in people's basements that need a dusting off and cranked through the speakers.

Brother Cane – S/T (Virgin - 1993) Southern Rock

In the early 1990's, there were still some quality artists putting out bluesy southern rock for the masses. Thanks in part to bands like The Black Crowes and Blues Traveler at the front of the line. Brother Cane was one of those bands that were also making a lot of noise. Their blend of blues, southern and hard rock turned some heads, and when 1993's debut album came out, they were a band on the rise. The record had three radio hits in "Got No Shame," "Hard Act To Follow" and "That Don't Satisfy Me." Those songs among the other tracks on this album set the bar for the band, and they continued through the 90s posting a few more hits like "And Fools Shine On" and "I Lie In The Bed I Make." However, much of the staying power of Brother Cane has been on the decline, which is unfair to an excellent band. Unlike the Black Crowes and Blues Traveler, who still garner radio airplay, Brother Cane is no longer on the radar, and it's hard to understand why. Their debut was a popular gem at the time but has fallen away from many listeners that surely would appreciate them.

The Cars – Panorama (Elektra - 1980) New Wave

By the time The Cars released *Panorama* in 1980, they were already one of, if not the premier new wave band out of the US. In fact, are there any bad songs on the debut record or *Candy-O*? Panorama focused on being more experimental than the previous releases and other than "Touch And Go," there are no other songs that found their way to a radio station playlist. There is a lot to like about *Panorama*. Tracks like "Don't Tell Me No," "Running To You" and "Up And Down" have the signature Cars sound, but the tracks seem to have more of a stripped-down approach and are more aggressive. If you listen to *Candy-O* and then play *Panorama*, you will tell instantly how all the songs are just darker and not as punchy. However, it fits the attitude and creativity they were looking for. Perhaps this takes away from the more pop-oriented tracks that fans and radio enjoyed. While *Panorama* still managed to go Platinum, it was sort of a risk for the band. Fear not, The Cars get back on track in 1981 with *Shake It Up*.

Cats In Boots – Kicked & Klawed (EMI - 1989) Hard Rock

While artists like Loudness and EZO were trying to claim a piece of the hard rock scene in the US, being a band from Japan did not always translate into major success (if ever). Sure, both groups were highly talented, but there was something wrong as to why neither of those bands made a significant move. Then there were Cats In Boots, who were a distinctly different band from Japan. The group itself was comprised of members from both the US and Japan. More of a collaboration of sorts but it worked, and of course, EMI would pick up the band and drop them into late 80s hair band mania. The result was *Kicked & Klawed*, a fast-paced, high energy album which featured amazing vocals, guitar work, and an impressive rhythm section. Standout tracks include "Shotgun Sally," "Nine Lives (Save Me)," and "Long, Long Way from Home." The band made the most of the opportunity as "Shotgun Sally" got some MTV play. However, in the end, they were sadly just another one and done as the 80s closed. Cats In Boots was definitely one band that slipped away without much notice.

Cheap Trick – All Shook Up (Epic-1980) Classic Rock

Rockford, IL foursome Cheap Trick was a blip on the radar before their massive live album *At Budokan* came out in 1978. The band had released three albums in the US, but in Japan, they were the Beatles and that success translated back to the states. In fact, Cheap Trick's fourth release *Dream Police* needed to be pushed back due to the success of *At Budokan*. *Dream Police* would follow *Budokan* into the Top 5 on the album charts, and there was a lot of buzz for the next release. After having Tom Werman as their producer for all their previous records, they brought in famous Beatles producer Sir George Martin to handle the controls. The one thing that made Cheap Trick great was that they were never afraid to change up their sound or experiment. Go back and listen to all the recordings before *All Shook Up* and you will see how each record is different. The band would see many of their fans turn their nose to this record. However, the Cheap Trick formula of quirky, hard power pop is always evident. The ace in the hole is always vocalist Robin Zander, who could sing the phone book and sound awesome. From the opening track "Stop This Game" which was the only charting single off this release, the hard rockers "Just Got Back," "Baby Loves To Rock" and the new wave style rocker "High Priest Of Rhythmic Noise," Cheap Trick put together a release that covers all terrain. It's amazing how songs like the hard ballad "Can't Stop It But I'm Gonna Try" and "World's Greatest Lover" were never released as singles? My only guess is that people came down from cranking up "I Want You To Want Me" and were turned off by the direction the band was going. The group has continued to release records in their Hall of Fame career, 17 and counting. However, when it comes to the ultimate diamond in the rough, look no further than *All Shook Up*.

Rick Neilsen and Robin Zander of Cheap Trick (photo by Byron Crowley)

Child's Play – Rat Race (Chrysalis - 1990) Hard Rock

While Kix may have been the most dominate hard rock band from Balti-more in the 1980's, the city also produced Child's Play. Of course, like many other artists who released albums in 1990 and forward, they were a band with a great sound but would be more of a blip on the radar and a record in the bargain bin. With *Rat Race*, Child's Play had a raw hard rock sound where other bands that were the top tier bands were either glam to the max or sleazed out rock like Guns N Roses, L.A. Guns and the like. *Rat Race* had a blues flavor and was not overproduced, which makes this record stand out. There were some excellent vocals and harmonies throughout this disc. Just give a listen to "My Bottle," "Good Old Rock N Roll" and "Damned If I Do" for an album that contains a group of songs that bring the party. Sorry to see that this band did not materialize into something bigger. Maybe it's the wrong place, wrong time. The band would eventually break up, but some members would find some success in other groups like SR-71 and Charm City Devils.

Christine McVie – S/T (Warner Brothers - 1984) Classic Rock

At their peak, Fleetwood Mac was one of the most popular and recognized bands on the planet. Of course, it wasn't until Lindsey Buckingham, and Stevie Nicks came into the fold that the group would generate dozens of hits and have some of the most popular albums of all time. One reason for that success was the 3-part harmonies and lead vocals of Buckingham, Nicks and Christine McVie, who had some very successful songs like "You Make Loving Fun" and "Over My Head." In the early 80s, all three mem-bers were putting out solo releases. Of course, Stevie Nicks would become the most popular of the three. Buckingham would have some hits of his own, and finally, in 1984, McVie would release her solo album. The album itself is a fine work showing Christine in her own element, without the rest of the band. Let's face it, Christine finally gets to break out of the back of this threesome and stand out on her own. She would have "Got A Hold on Me" as a Top 10 hit and other tracks like "Love Will Show Us How" and "I'm The One" that were excellent musical elements of classic/pop rock craft. The unfortunate thing for McVie is that she always took a backseat to Stevie, and that is just unfair. I'm sure many that would say that Christine McVie was the better vocalist of the band but apparently wasn't as flashy as Nicks' gypsy persona. Clearly a case of image over substance. This solo record is one that has genuinely been forgotten over time.

Circle Jerks – VI (Combat-1987) Punk Rock

Circle Jerks are one of the premier punk rock bands of the 80s. Rising from the punk rock tree of Black Flag and Redd Kross, they laid down the groundwork for future groups in both the punk and hardcore movements from California. Some of those bands include The Offspring and Pennywise. By the time we got to *VI*, the band was beginning to phase out. In the early days, the group was pure punk and even scored an appearance in the film *Repo Man*. In 1985, they would release *Wonderful*, which would branch more into hard rock/metal (does anyone remember "American Heavy Metal Weekend"?). In 1987, vocalist Keith Morris and guitarist Greg Hetson may have put together their best work. The songs were fired up punk rock with tracks like "I'm Alive," "All Wound Up" and CCR's "Fortunate Son" that showed the band's radio potential. While heavier numbers like "Beat Me Senseless," "Status Clinger" and "Protection" would make all the punks get into the pit. The band would take a 5-year hiatus and return in 1994. They would sign to a major label, have Debbie Gibson guest sing, and it probably was not the best of returns. It would have been great to see what the band could have been if not for a break.

Circus Of Power – Vices (RCA - 1990) Hard Rock

Around 1987, a band known as Guns N Roses came on the scene and changed the game for all the "glam metal" artists. GNR was edgier and more like a biker band then hairspray and makeup. Record labels were signing anything close to what GNR brought to the table. On the west coast, it was in the form of L.A. Guns and Faster Pussycat. On the East Coast, Skid Row and a New York band known as Circus Of Power. With their 1988 debut, Circus of Power made some noise, and in 1990, they would release *Vices*. A heavy dose of edgy blues metal that had plenty of power, in your face straight up attitude and for a New York band, some southern vibes (must be that slide guitar). Some of the tracks that stand out include "Gates Of Love," "Two River Highway" and "Last Call Rosie." Not sure what happened but *Vices* failed to chart and compared to some of the bands that were coming out, it's almost criminal. The group would release one more record before calling it quits in 1995. The band recently has reformed and published new music in 2018.

City Boy – S/T (Renaissance Recordings - 1976) Classic Rock

So, before Robert John "Mutt" Lange was tweaking the controls for artists like AC/DC, Ratt, Nickelback and his ex-wife Shania Twain, he had to have a starting point. So that brings us to the English rock band City Boy, who released their debut album in 1976. City Boy was your basic melodic rock band with branches going out to pop, folk, prog/psychedelic, and even funk stylings. Songs like "Oddball Dance," "Sunset Boulevard" and "The Greatest Story Ever Told" are just a few sample tracks that show a band that refuses to sound the same every track yet find a way to keep it all tied together. The group would continue to use Lange as a producer and have some success but would never become a household name. By 1981, they would disband. For Lange, it was just the beginning of his future.

Guitarist/Vocalist Steve Broughton had some success working with Cyndi Lauper (co-writer of She-Bop) and as a VP for Jive Records, gave us Britney Spears, NSYNC, and Backstreet Boys. You're welcome.

Clutch – The Elephant Riders (Columbia - 1998) Stoner Rock

One of the top tier bands of the stoner rock genre, Clutch was signed to Columbia and released *The Elephant Riders* in 1998. Produced by the legendary Jack Douglass (The Who, Aerosmith, Blue Oyster Cult), this album should have been a slam dunk just by association. With *The Elephant Riders*, Clutch was combining their brand of stoner rock with metal, and funk. This combination was evident on tracks like "The Soapmakers," "The Dragonfly" and the title track. *The Elephant Riders* should have been a more important album when it was released. It failed to crack the Top 100, and the band was dumped from the label. Over time, Clutch has had a very loyal cult following and continue to release albums and tour. For those just getting into the band or the stoner rock/metal genre need to preview this album.

Concrete Blonde – S/T (I.R.S.-1986)

Most people when you speak of Concrete Blonde will automatically say "Joey," the smash hit single from their 1990 album *Bloodletting*. Only the real fan will remember how awesome the 1986 debut is. The band was a three piece at the time, and vocalist/bassist Johnette Napolitano was the main songwriter. At the time of hair bands and new wave, Concrete Blonde was carving a way for the mainstream bands of the 1990's. Concrete Blonde was different than your normal rock band, with well-written songs and Napolitano's haunting and melodic vocals. While many of their songs were of a slower tempo with a pop element like "Dance Along The Edge" and "True," they had some rockers like the punkish "Still In Hollywood," "Over Your Shoulder" and "Your Haunted Head." While "True" made the radio charts, they only made a small dent at the time. 1989's *Free* would take them a little further before "Joey" became the band's radio staple.

Core (photo courtesy of Jeremy Johnson)

Core – St. Judas Day Parade (2010 – Self Released) Hard Rock

This three-piece from North Dakota might be the only band from that great state on the list. Back in 2010, Core self-released *St. Judas Day Parade*, and it will blow people out of the way. With elements of hard rock, prog, and modern rock stylings, they were a band that should have been on the rise. Vocalist/guitarist Jeremy Johnson has a vocal structure that is unique and a cross between Claudio Sanchez of Coheed and Cambria and Raine Maida of Our Lady Peace. With songs like "Hate Me Harder," "Live Forever" and "Obscene," it was no wonder why Core was opening for dozens of national acts throughout the Midwest. Despite eventually getting on a label and releasing *Broken Heart Syndrome* in 2015, the band has never gotten the true opportunity to get out of its regional scene. Which means that millions of modern hard rock fans are missing one of the truly great sounding bands to come out from 2010 to now.

Corrosion Of Conformity – America's Volume Dealer (Sanctuary - 2000) Metal

C.O.C.'s long history has placed them into a variety of genres. They were one of the first bands known as crossover along with Suicidal Tendencies and D.R.I. Eventually, their punk/hardcore style would cross into thrash/sludge metal, and when *Deliverance* arrived in 1994, it was the sludge/stoner/southern rock sound that C.O.C. embraced, thanks to the talents of guitarist and now lead vocalist Pepper Keenan. The band marched on in the 90s with another solid release in *Wiseblood*. By the time *America's Volume Dealer* came out in 2000, C.O.C. was full-on southern metal. This appeared to have turned away some fans of the band, but for those that stuck around, they know that this CD is a hidden gem. C.O.C. did not ditch sludge, they just focused more on the southern rock stylings and placed that to the front of their songwriting. While there is plenty of heaviness in "Congratulation's Song" and "Who's Got The Fire," I believe some fans were taken back by how much the band had gone full-on southern rock. This is probably most evident in the southern rock ballad "Stare Too Long," complete with acoustic guitars and special guest Warren Haynes on slide guitar. I think one lyric from "Stare Too Long" says it best for *America's Volume Dealer*, "but I don't care, cause I've got nothing to lose."

Crimson Glory – Transcendence (MCA - 1988) Progressive Metal

Towards the late 80s, progressive rock/metal was starting to change shape and gain popularity. While bands like Rush, Yes and Genesis were becoming more radio-friendly, there were bands like Queensryche, Dream Theater and Fates Warning that were bringing in a new wave of progressive music. Another lesser known band also a part of the genre was Crimson Glory. While their formation only really lasted until 1992, they had released three albums during their main run but may have been known more for the silver masks they wore instead of their musical skills. In 1988, they released *Transcendence*, which showcases a band that should have been as big as the previously mentioned bands. They could be heavy, go acoustic and the vocal talents of Midnight are some of the most overlooked period. From the tempo changing "Painted Skies," the powerful "Lonely" and the fist pounding "Where Dragons Rule," it's got all the great ingredients of prog metal. Soaring vocals? Check! Dual guitar attack? Check! The musical direction that takes you everywhere and does not keep you in the same old place? Yes, *Transcendence* does that. The biggest problem. Queensryche was making the beginning of its run as top band of the Progressive Rock/Metal scene and Crimson Glory at times may have reminded too many people of the Seattle band. The group took a back seat and never really got their significant opportunity to break out. Crimson Glory took a hiatus in 2013, and former vocalist Todd La Torre (2010-2013) replaced Geoff Tate in Queensryche. Maybe the similarities are closer than we think between the two bands?

The Cult – Beyond Good and Evil (Atlantic - 2001) Hard Rock

Say what you want about The Cult, but a lack of diversity with their sound is not something that can be said about Ian Astbury and Billy Duffy. A band that went from goth punk, new wave, AC/DC style hard rock to eventually a combination of all of their techniques by the time they released 1989's, *Sonic Temple*. Of course, when the 90s grunge explosion took over the rock scene, The Cult was around, but releases like *Ceremony* and the self-titled CD did not pack the same punch. Eventually, The Cult would disband until the release of *Beyond Good And Evil* in 2001. While it does not climb the charts like *Sonic Temple*, the template is there for what worked on that record. First, they brought Bob Rock in to produce, and drummer Matt Sorum makes his return to the band. This is by far the heaviest release The Cult has put out, and Astbury and Duffy are on top of their game musically and lyrically. Beginning with the charging rocker "Rise," "The Saint" and "War (The Process), The Cult had something to say and wanted to let everyone know that they were not a band from the 80s to be pushed aside. Billy Duffy is also one of the most underrated guitarists in rock, while Astbury shows excellent vocal range throughout this release.

D-E

D-A-D – No Fuel Left For The Pilgrims (Warner Bros - 1989) Hard Rock

D-A-D is hugely popular in Denmark, their home country. During the Glam Metal 80s, the band previously known as Disneyland After Dark set their sights on America. D-A-D was a melodic hard rock band with a little bit of an edge. *No Fuel Left For The Pilgrims* should have been a slam dunk. The lead single "Sleeping My Day Away" was perfect for radio and MTV. While other standout tracks like the heavier "Jihad" and The Cult sounding "Girl Nation" put this band in a perfect situation for success, it never materialized. The band would release *Riskin It All* in 1991, but after that, it was a return to focus in Europe and their home country, where they have three #1 charting albums.

D.A.D. (photo by Deborah Feingold)

The Dandy Warhols – The Dandy Warhols Come Down (Capitol - 1997) Alternative Rock

Here is a band that can be classified as one of the most underrated bands in rock history. The Dandy Warhols are an alternative rock/power pop band from Oregon and in most circles defined to a cult following. Which is ok because it was everyone else's loss. While many listeners might not have gotten it, David Bowie and Andy Taylor of Duran Duran were two people that did over the years. The release of *Come Down*, the band's 2nd, was to be the breakout for the band. While grunge was on its way to pop and Nu Metal was just starting to take shape, *Come Down* was a breath of fresh air for the true alternative rockers. Most of the charm to the band's sound is where many songs tend to go into a repetitive spin, that only puts you more into a trance of their musical landscape. These were very well-structured alt-rock songs where nothing dominates and overshadows, putting you in a place where all the instruments and vocals are one, and you are never focusing on anything individual. This is evident on tracks like "Boys Better," the jangle-pop western "Minnesoter" and "Cool As Kim Deal." It's also amazing nobody got hooked on "Not If You're The Last Junkie On Earth" when it debuted on radio or MTV. I'm sure most of the alternative rock bands today should be thanking The Dandy Warhols. Let's face it, Dandy's did it first.

Jim Santora with Peter Holdstrom of Dandy Warhols (photo by Leroy Hickman)

Danko Jones – Never Too Loud (Bad Taste - 2008) Hard Rock

While Danko Jones is very popular in Canada and Europe, in the US, they seem to be one of the more underappreciated bands. Outside of a few minor hits like "First Kiss" and "Full Of Regret," this three-piece hard rock unit has never really caught on. One fine example of this is 2008's *Never Too Loud*. Danko Jones is where Motorhead meets Thin Lizzy. A perfect combination of heavy three-piece rock, melodic, yet not afraid to get very aggressive and loud. On *Never Too Loud*, it's an album that stays true to that combination. Standout tracks include the straight-up power rocker "Code Of The Road," the step-down melodic sing-along rocker "Take Me Home" and "Still In High School." Lyrically, Danko Jones is a sex machine and is not afraid to show that in their lyrics. This album is between the records where they have scored some minor hits. How this album did not get any significant attention is beyond anyone's imagination. A truly underrated band indeed.

Dead Boys – We Have Come For Your Children (Sire - 1978) Punk

While there are more prominent names in the history of punk, it's hard not to recognize the Dead Boys for their contribution. This punk band from Cleveland was one of the early pioneers of American punk music. Of course, while punk was just beginning to explode and groups like the Ramones, Sex Pistols, and others were getting more visibility, Dead Boys were true punk in the traditional sense. With their 2nd release *We Have Come For Your Children*, they display pure rock energy in their music. It's raw, aggressive and while it can be as accessible as anything the Ramones or the Stooges were doing during that time, it seems that they would come up just a little short from being amongst the popular bands in the scene. There are some great songs on this album, beginning with the opening track "3rd Generation Nation". This song sets the tone for any rebellious punk. Another standout is "I Don't Want to Be No Catholic Boy" display a tune of a true punk not being a good responsible kid. Other songs like "Calling on You" start with clean guitar but then morph into true punk rock fashion. While other bands from their scene would eventually move into the 80s and get sort of lumped into New Wave, the Dead Boys would not make it out of the 70s after this release. While their debut *Young, Loud and Snotty* is considered a punk masterpiece, *We Have Come for Your Children* is a good follow up that does not get nearly the praise it deserves.

Detective – It Takes One To Know One (Swan Song - 1977) Rock

There is something in the water with so many of these underrated and underappreciated bands from the 70s. This would be the case with Detective and their second album *It Takes One To Know One*. The album cover of the group does not match what this band sounds like. Detective is a 5-piece band that is stripped down back to basics rock and can lay down elements of hard rock, blues, and funk rock into their sound. At times, you can hear a little bit of Led Zeppelin in the mix (they were label mates), and vocalist Michael Des Barres has a cross mix of Robert Plant meets Rod Stewart when he sings. This is one album that is not hard on the ears and appears to be very forgotten. Tracks like "Competition," "Betcha Won't Dance" and "Help Me Up" are highlights to a band that needs to be heard. The band toured with Kiss in support of the album and almost worked with John Mellencamp on some songs for another record. The group disbanded and disappeared without a trace, except for this underrated gem that's worth digging up. On another note, Tony Kaye of Yes was a keyboardist for the band while Michael Des Barres would become vocalist of Power Station after Robert Palmer's departure but never released any music with the group.

Deuce – Nine Lives (Five Seven - 2012) Rap Rock

Deuce got his start with the rap-rock/crunkcore band Hollywood Undead as one of the rapper/vocalists. He left after their first album in and apparently the feud still burns to this day. In 2012, Deuce was back with *Nine Lives*. This album is raw, full of raunch and is brilliant. Just when you think you're getting just a full-on rap record like another Vanilla Ice clone, Deuce brings the rock, gets deep lyrically and can get heavy on the electronic beats. Songs like the powerful "America," the sex-crazed, drinking anthem "I Came To Party," and the come together song of "The One," weave the rap and rock in ways that people who enjoy both would appreciate what they hear. There is some weirdness, like the lyrical stylings of Jeffree Starr but it all fits on *Nine Lives*. This album jumped in and out of the Billboard charts like a cup of coffee. Most people completely missed what Deuce was throwing down.

Devo – Something For Everybody (Warner Brothers - 2010) New Wave

Devo was probably the most recognizable of the punk/new wave bands breaking out in the late 70s early 1980's. They had a combination of punk, synth, pop and just plain weird. This only added to the intrigue of the band. Their musical breakthrough was "Whip It," released in 1981. Towards the end of the 80s, Devo sort of fell out of favor like so many other new wave bands did with the 90s alternative rock scene taking shape. The band would drift in and out of the 90s and 2000's, with vocalist/keyboardist Mark Mothersbaugh having a very successful career composing music for various movies and television shows. With no new music in twenty years, Devo would finally return with *Something For Everybody* in 2010. Now when you are looking for a band to reinvent themselves, this album does the opposite and could slide into their previous catalog with no problems. The band had a way to take various synth style instruments and make it cool while their trademark humorous off the wall lyrics are front and center. Beginning with the opening track "Fresh" which will bring hardcore fans back to the 1980's all over again. Other songs like "What We Do" have a techno groove that gives the band a more modern feel and "Later Is Now" has a very melodic tone which may be a little out of the ordinary compared to the chaotic sounds the band amazingly put together 30+ years prior. This may not be an album that blew up the charts, but it is proof that Devo and their musical footprint never went away.

Devo (photo by Janet Macoska)

The Dictators – Manifest Destiny (Asylum - 1977) Punk Rock

Coming from the same punk scene as The Ramones and having members who would eventually be parts of Twisted Sister and Manowar, The Dictators were a very talented band. With their 2nd album, *Manifest Destiny*, they show a combination of punk attitude with a melodic garage rock sound. On this album, some things set them apart from traditional punk. For example, The Dictators have a keyboard player, evident in songs like "Sleepin With The TV On," a more garage style ballad. Other songs like the galloping rocker "Science Has Gone Too Far," and the opening track

"Exposed" show a band that had so much more in common with Kiss and Nazareth along with traits of say the MC5 and The Stooges. The Dictators are one band that sort of gets lost in the shuffle outside of fans of early punk music. They are a band that had plenty to offer, despite not having ultimate success as say The Ramones and Talking Heads. They apparently showed as an evident influence for artists heading into the 80s and 90s.

Dinosaur jr – Your Living All Over Me (SST- 1987) Alternative Rock

In my early days of college radio, I got into some really cool bands. I stumbled upon Dinosaur jr (known as merely Dinosaur) when I was reading a review stating the band's sound was similar to Neil Young. I was indeed curious about checking out this record. *Your Living All Over Me* is a lo-fi rock masterpiece that shows how the music landscape was changing. Give tracks like "Kracked," "Raisins," and the headphone rattling jam "Sludgefeast" a listen and you can see how bands like Nirvana, Smashing Pumpkins and other 90s chart-toppers carved their sound. J. Mascis had a vocal tone very similar to Neil Young. The team of Mascis on guitar and vocals, Lou Barlow on bass and Murph on drums was loud and fierce. While this release was basically a college radio staple, Dinosaur jr would have to wait until 1991 for their first record to chart (Green Mind) and they have continued to chart ever since. You may have seen J. Mascis on the cover of *Spin* in 1993, basically calling him god. Before those days, they were just laying down the groundwork, and *Your Living All Over Me* is the first record you should be listening to from this band.

Dire Straits – Love Over Gold (Warner Brothers - 1982) Classic Rock

Dire Straits Mark Knopfler is a musical genius, and there are times where I do not believe he gets the credit he deserves. His melding of roots rock, jazz, folk, and blues is impressive based on his body of work, and it's a journey to go through his entire musical catalog, both with Dire Straits and his solo work. Of course, the band will always be remembered for 1985's *Brothers In Arms* and the "I Want My MTV" catch-phrase lyrics sung by Sting on the song "Money For Nothing." However, in 1982 they released *Love Over Gold*, an album that may be the best overall work from the band and the most overlooked outside of true fans. Opening with the stellar "Telegraph Road," which clocks in at almost 15 minutes is an absolute classic. Not to mention that Knopfler's guitar work truly stands out in this great arrangement. Other songs like "Industrial Disease" capture what we could see was going to become of "Money For Nothing" both musically and lyrically. The title track is another song that displays the intelligence of their music. *Love Over Gold* only consists of five songs, and most of those were too long for radio one would suppose. It's not that this album sold poorly because it would go platinum, but it would be hard to find the average person that knows Dire Straits to say they know anything from this album.

Dirty Looks – Turn Of The Screw (Atlantic - 1989) Hard Rock

For those not familiar with Dirty Looks, they have a Danish-born vocalist/guitarist who went from Erie Pa to California and eventually signed to Atlantic. Their debut *Cool From The Wire* was a great hard rock album that drew similarities to AC/DC for both the music and the obvious vocal talents of Henrik Ostergaard. While *Cool From The Wire* was the springboard for the band, the follow-up was supposed to be the next level of success. *Turn Of The Screw* has that definite AC/DC stomp to a modernized late 80s hard rock sound that of course gets lumped into the hair band sound of the time. From the rocking bounce of "Nobody Rides For Free," "Slammin To the Big Beat" to the stop and go melodic action of "L.A. Anna," this album should have contained multiple hits. Instead, this recording and the band pretty much became another 80s hair band casualty. They would continue to record but would never come close to any significant success, and Ostergaard's passing in 2010 brought a sad end to the band.

Dokken – Dysfunctional (Sony - 1995) Hard Rock

Dokken is one of the primary bands that kicked off the 80s hard rock era along with Motley Crue, Quiet Riot, and Ratt. These bands are the beginnings of what would become "hair metal." Despite their popularity, they still came off at times as a second-tier group even behind bands that followed them. Could it have been that their sound at times was even more melodic and heavier than their counterparts? You had the 1-2 punch with Don Dokken on vocals and George Lynch on guitar. That alone would have been enough. Add drummer Mick Brown and bassist Jeff Pilson on the back end, and this was one solid lineup. As the 80s moved on, there was plenty of friction in the band, which resulted in their eventual breakup. In 1995, after a seven-year hiatus, the classic lineup was back with *Dysfunctional*. This album was a surprise on the charts but faded as fast as it got there. Most traditional fans were not very keen on the direction of this record, that came off in parts as more grunge than the 80s hard rock they were used to. Which is a shame, because of songs like "Too High To Fly" flat out rock even without Lynch crushing out a guitar solo. There is also plenty of Don Dokken's vocals showing why he was one of the best voices of the 80s on tracks like "The Maze." Songs like "Shadows Of Life" and "Inside Looking Out" display some tremendous three-part harmonies from Dokken, Brown, and Pilson. Overall, this is one Dokken release that deserves a second listen.

Downset – Do We Speak A Dead Language (Mercury - 1996) Hardcore

West Coast hardcore/rap metal band Downset started in the late 80s and credited as one of the first hardcore punk bands to incorporate rap into their music. They signed to Mercury Records in 1994 and released their self-titled debut, featuring some powerful tracks like "Anger." In 1996, it was more of the same as they released *Do We Speak A Dead Language*. Downset was a band that had power, attitude and were just full throttle in every song. With songs like "Empower," "Eyes Shut Tight" and "Pocket Full Of Fatcaps" they show a band that wrote about life on the streets and were not afraid to put their feelings in their lyrics. Musically, they produced earth pounding hardcore with funk elements. Downset also falls into the beginnings of nu-metal but does not get into the discussion of other bands like Korn and Deftones. Had they been more in the mix with those bands at the time, perhaps *Do We Speak A Dead Language* would be more than just an underrated release.

Dread Zeppelin – Un-Led-Ed (I.R.S. - 1990) Reggae Rock

So, what do you get when you cross Led Zeppelin, Elvis and Reggae music? You get Dread Zeppelin, one of the most prominent oddball sounds you may ever hear. Not sure if they were a true Reggae band or using this for comedic purposes but it's genius. In 1990, they released *Un-Led-Ed*. Let me explain the formula for those who have never heard this band. You take Led Zeppelin songs, and the vocalist is Elvis (sounds/dresses like him), and all songs are sung in that style. Musically, you get Led Zeppelin if they were an actual reggae band. Standout tracks showcase their style include "Heartbreaker (At The End Of Lonely Street)/Heartbreak Hotel," "Whole Lotta Love" and "I Can't Quit You, Baby." This might not be an album up everyone's alley. In fact, some people might even feel insulted that a band would turn Led Zep and Elvis music into a mockery. But maybe that's the point. To just put a lighter approach to some favorite tracks and have some fun. If that was the goal, then the concept was a success.

Drivin N Cryin – Whisper Tames The Lion (Island - 1988) Alternative Rock

The state of Georgia, particularly the cities of Atlanta and Athens have brought us some great musical artists over the years. In the late 70s and 80s, there were the likes of R.E.M. and the B-52's that gained in popularity. Then there was Drivin N Cryin, which while an almost unknown to most people, they were one of the most popular bands in the south. When they released *Whisper Tames The Lion* in 1988, they were a hard band to classify, and that was track by track. The title track was a straight up three-chord rocker, which was followed by a bluegrass style number in "Catch The Wind." When I first heard this, I was confused but wanted to listen to more. The styles continued to weave back and forth including some more R.E.M. inspired numbers and tracks that morphed into a combination of alternative rock meets southern rock. Songs like the heavy rocker "Power-house" and the somber "Check Your Tears At The Door" show a band that was not afraid to play it anything other than right up the middle. The group would embrace more southern rock and hard rock in later releases, but *Whisper* remains an authentic listening experience. Also, to note, Kevn Kinney's lyrics are some of the most visual words put to music. File under hidden gem.

Duran Duran – Big Thing (EMI - 1988) New Wave

During the 1980's, there was a lot of music, and increased genres were starting to come into play. Everything from glam metal, new wave and the birth of alternative/modern rock was becoming a thing. One thing was for sure, Duran Duran was one of the biggest bands of the time. Duran Duran was looking at the ever-changing musical direction, and in 1988, the group shifted from its new wave/dance-pop styles to synthpop. While this album has its critics, and of course the songs from *Big Thing* are probably not the top 5 Duran Duran songs that come to mind. It still is an excellent listen and shows a band that was not afraid to take a step in a different direction. Standout tracks like "All She Wants Is" and "I Don't Want Your Love" were successful enough at the time to get people on the dance floor. While "Do You Believe In Shame?" was one song from *Big Thing* that tracks back to a more familiar sound that fans were familiar with. The band would go back to more of their traditional sound as they moved into the 90s, but *Big Thing* is the one album from the group that they were not afraid to step out of the box and take a risk.

Earshot – The Silver Lining (Fontana - 2008) Hard Rock

When Tool broke out in the 1990's, their sound was so influential, it was hard not to find bands that would adapt pieces of what they assembled. Bands like Chevelle and 10 Years come to mind. When Earshot came onto the scene in the early 2000's, it looked like they could be at the forefront of bands that had this Tool influenced sound. Their first two albums did decently and spawned some minor hits. What was bigger is that the band's music was on several video games, which only helped their reach to fans. When *The Silver Lining* was released, this should have been an album that helped them reach new heights. Top tracks include the melodic and lighter (term used loosely) "Misunderstood," "Closer" and "Pushing To Shove."

Earshot is a band that is technical, yet still melodic and powerful. However, many people missed the boat on this band, and it is impressive considering how the other artists we mentioned in this discussion continued to perform well with the masses.

Eclipse – Bleed & Scream (Frontiers - 2012) Hard Rock

While glam or hair metal came and went in the 80s to early 90s, there were still a few bands trying to carry the torch. In the late 2000's, there had become a revival of sorts with some of the old school still touring and releasing albums attempting to capture that period. If you go to Europe, some of that flair has never gone away. In fact, it's embraced. Take Swedish band Eclipse for example. Beginning with their first release in 2001, they have become part of a wave of newer bands that stayed true to the 80s brand of hard rock, with a modern twist of course. In 2012, they released the fantastic *Bleed & Scream*, which sounds like a more energetic version of Europe. A swirling blend of melodic vocals, heavy guitars, strong bottom end bass, drums, and synths to add to the musical spectrum. The title track and "Wake Me Up" are strong in your face melodic hard rock, while "About To Break" is more of the traditional power ballad that will make you think, 1989 but it's 2012. Eclipse is a band that hasn't had much of an opportunity to break into the US outside of an underground following. They are a band that precisely captures the energy of that era of music, and for any fan of the 80s looking for groups that continue to hold the torch, Eclipse and *Bleed & Scream* is one of those albums.

Electric Light Orchestra – On The Third Day (UA-1973) Classic Rock

When most people pose the question, when did you first get turned onto rock music, my answer usually is in 1976 when I got a copy of Kiss *Destroyer* for Christmas. Truth is, my first introduction to rock music is a classic, yet unknown album from Electric Light Orchestra titled *On The Third Day*. As a young kid, I found this album in a collection my mother had that she won in a radio station contest. In my opinion, one of the most refreshing albums of all time. For one, Jeff Lynne is a musical genius that does not always get the credit he rightfully deserves. Second, how many bands can rock as a seven-piece complete with a cello, violin, and Moog to go along with the traditional guitar, bass, drums, and vocals. *On The Third Day* is a vibrant musical landscape. A combination of late-era Beatles meets prog rock meets orchestra. Most of the tracks fall on a softer side of rock with Lynne's soothing vocals and excellent string work. Tracks like "Showdown" and "New World Rising/Ocean Breakup" are evidence of that. Even the one true rock track, "Ma-Ma-Ma Belle" is a remarkable display of what this band could do with all the instruments involved. This is a perfect description of music as art.

Elf – S/T (Purple Records - 1972) Blues Rock

Ronnie James Dio is a legend. The voice of bands like Rainbow, Black Sabbath and Heaven N Hell. Not to mention his work in his own group, Dio. He even has a song about him from Jack Black's Tenacious D and had a cameo in the movie *Tenacious D and the Pick of Destiny*. Before that, many people don't know that Dio had been singing as a teenager back in the 50s and 60s. In the late 60s, Elf is created but do not get their first break until their debut album was released in 1972. Dio is not just lead vocalist but plays bass on the record. One note, on this album, Dio goes by

46

his birth name Ronnie Padavona. Musically, this album is straight up 70s blues-rock, with parts of it heavy at times. You will not find any songs about dragons, rainbows or men on silver mountains. Not yet anyhow. What you will find out is that Dio, (I mean Padavona) has a great voice and as proven by his future endeavors, he can sing any style you put in front of him. Standout songs include "Hoochie Coochie Lady," the ballad "Never More" and "Sit Down Honey (Everything Will Be Alright)," which show a band that plays the blues and can flat out boogie when they want to. Elf would put out a few more albums and eventually most of the group would join Richie Blackmore of Deep Purple in his band Rainbow. The rest is the beginning of history for one Ronnie Padavona aka DIO!

F-G

Fair To Midland – Fables From A Mayfly: What I Tell You Three Times Is True (Universal - 2007) Progressive Rock

The exciting part of prog rock bands is how they adapted over the years, continuing to bring more objectivity to the music as well as creativity. By the mid-2000's, many prog rock bands were also being lumped into the tail end of what was nu-metal and even alternative rock/metal. Found by Serj Tankian of System of a Down, Fair to Midland was a band that had unique and original ideas in a sea of groups that were all beginning to sound alike. With their third release *Fables From A Mayfly*, this was a band that clearly had their own objectives and were not going to just go with what every other artist was doing. Beginning with their biggest song "Dance of the Manatee," full of blistering guitars, prog-style arrangements and the incredible vocals of Darroh Sudderth," who could sing in a weird vibrato one-minute, soaring highs next and not to be outdone, some deep metallic vocals in the bridge. This is just the opening track, and after one listen, you're hooked. Other tracks like "Tall Tales Sound Like Sour Grapes" start with violin, but before you think you're listening to a Kansas track, the metallic guitars are front and center while Sudderth's vocals grab you again like a pied piper. "Upgrade Brigade" is another track full of metallic thunder and soothing progressive tones. Fair to Midland would release another album in 2011, but nothing much has happened since. While *Fables From A Mayfly* did manage to break the Billboard 200 at the time of its release, Fair To Midland is one of the most original bands to come around in rock that did not get embraced, as this album proves they deserved.

Fastway – S/T (CBS - 1983) Hard Rock

Fastway was intended to be a supergroup featuring "Fast" Eddie Clarke of Motorhead and Pete Way of UFO. Way would leave the band and eventually form Waysted, leaving Clarke with then unknown vocalist Dave King. The Fastway debut album is truly a rock n roll treasure. This may very well be one of the most underappreciated straight-up rock albums. From the opening riffs of "Easy Livin," this was a band running on all cylinders and no chance of slowing down. King's vocals are a major highlight throughout. His Robert Plant type voice is dominant and shows great range on songs like "Another Day" and the dark number "Heft." Of course, in 1983, the whole glam metal scene had not exploded yet, so bands like Fastway were still sort of late 70s leftovers that were up and comers. For Fastway, that could be the reason they didn't have more success after this first record (and this debut should have been much bigger). As the 80s rolled forward, Fastway tried to meld with what was going on and did not have much success. By 1990, it was pretty much over for the band. King would reinvent himself and is now best known as the vocalist and leader of the Celtic band Flogging Molly.

Firehose – If'n (SST - 1987) Alternative Rock

From the ashes of the punk band, The Minutemen become Firehose. A three-piece rock band with a flash of funk and some humor when applied to lyrics at times. In 1987, the group would release their second album *If'n*. Firehose was one of the standards of college rock radio at the time, and *If'n* did not disappoint. Standout tracks include the funky "Making The Freeway" the mocking of "For the Singer of R.E.M." and the alternative rock gem "Windmilling." All of the songs feature one of the most underrated bass players around in Mike Watt. Columbia Records would snatch the band up which would result in two albums in 1991 and 1993 for the label, but they never come close to what they did with *If'n* in 1987. *If'n* is still an unknown classic for many.

Flyleaf – Between The Stars (Loud and Proud - 2014) Hard Rock

Coming out in the late 2000's as a huge rock success story, Flyleaf broke some significant ground with their debut album with songs like "All Around Me" and "I'm So Sick." After three albums, vocalist Lacey Strum exited the band, and for album #4, Kristen May would become the new vocalist. The result was 2014's *Between The Stars*, which is a brilliant album. The band at this point in their career were not as heavy as their debut, but this was gradually happening per album. May's vocals paired with the band's sound is magic. May's vocals had a certain Hayley Williams of Paramore feel but make no mistake, Kristen May is solid. Standout tracks include "Well Of Lies," "Marionette" and "Set Me On Fire." Despite the great sounds, Flyleaf puts out on this album, it appears that most fans had moved on from the band. They performed moderately on the charts and radio. As of this review, May had left the group. Meanwhile, Strum stepped out on her own as a solo performer. So, the future of Flyleaf is floating in the air at this point.

The Forecast – In The Shadow Of Two Gunman (Victory - 2006) Alternative Rock

Sometimes miscategorized as an emo band, The Forecast was a four-piece Midwestern band with more of roots-driven sound than pretty much all the groups they were associated with on their label when they signed to Victory. They were complete with 3-part harmonies and almost an alternative country sound. That does not mean that they didn't have a little bit of edge in their music. When 2005's *Late Night Conversations* was released, things looked to be moving in the right direction with the band. Victory was riding an intense wave of bands like Hawthorne Heights, so when *In The Shadow Of Two Gunman* was released in 2006, it should have been met with tremendous fanfare? That did not happen, the album failed to gain a lot of steam, and it's hard to comprehend why. Perhaps it's that a band like The Forecast were unable to stand out in the rock of the new millennium. Beginning with the country style, "Some Things Never Change." This song perhaps in another era would have been a huge hit, complete with some great harmonies. Not to be confused as roots style band, they also bring a rocking sound in tracks like "A Fist Fight For Our Fathers," where harmonies are there right along with the loud guitars. Another track, "And We All Return To Our Roots," while a little scaled back, still flat out rocks, and the male/female vocal tradeoffs are what make the song. After this release, the band would leave Victory and despite a few releases, have fallen off into oblivion.

Fu Manchu – King Of The Road (Mammoth - 2000) Stoner Rock

If there is one genre of rock that does not get a lot of respect, it's stoner rock. Over the last 20+ years, there have been so many great bands that have helped shape the genre (Monster Magnet, Kyuss, The Sword) but in the end, have never been listed among the top tier rock bands. Fu Manchu is undoubtedly one of these bands that throughout the 90s and 2000's helped carry the torch of stoner rock. In 2000, they would release *King Of The Road*, a fantastic record full of loud amps and fuzz, which require it to be cranked up to maximum levels. With songs like bottom end rattler "Over The Edge," "Hell On Wheels" and "No Dice," there is no mistaking Fu Manchu from any other band. There is a very 70s style in their sound mixed in with some late 80s punk. Infectious grooves from front to back, *King Of The Road* will have hooked you into cruising the highway or kicking back with some beers on the couch. Fu Manchu is an underrated band that never disappoints.

Game Theory – Lolita Nation (Enigma-1987) Alternative Rock

Some bands are underrated. Then there is Game Theory. Probably one of the most overlooked and underappreciated bands on the planet. They were an 80s alternative rock/power pop five (or sometimes four) piece that could be compared to a West Coast version of R.E.M. or a modern rock version of Fleetwood Mac. Either way, vocalist/guitarist Scott Miller was a genius in his own right between the lyrics and song structure, which at times were a combination of pop meets prog rock. This may have been the band's Achilles heel. Miller and his band were not ones to jump ship and become pop darlings like others from their California scene (Bangles), but they would have a cult following with the 27-track double album *Lolita Nation*. Some of the press used words like gutsiest, ambitious and bizarre and they were not far off point. *Lolita Nation* showed that this band could be pop, alternative rock, prog, display some heavy riffs when needed and just pure weirdness at times. It still boggles the mind why songs like "Nothing New," "The Real Sheila" and "Dripping With Looks" were not instant hits. While *Lolita Nation* was getting plenty of college radio airplay, that's where the story ends. One more record would follow before Game Theory would disband, and Miller would form another underrated group in The Loud Family. Maybe they were ahead of their time, or maybe *Lolita Nation* was meant to be an underground treasure.

Game Theory (photo by Robert Toren)

The Godfathers – Birth, School, Work, Death (Epic - 1988) Alternative Rock

In the mid to late 80s, there was a 2nd wave of new wave bands coming over from the U.K. One of those bands was The Godfathers who were more of a guitar/bass/drums rock band than synth new wave. In 1988, they would release *Birth, School, Work, Death*, a collection of catchy rock numbers with equal parts new wave and punk thrown in for good measure. The title track is clearly the one song that got attention on both college radio and MTV for a moment. Other songs like the upbeat "If I Only Had Time" and the moody punk-influenced "Cause I Said So" are the mix throughout this album. The Godfathers would not do much after this release, and it was unfortunate because the title track alone should have been a colossal anthem during its time.

The Godz – S/T (RCA - 1978) Hard Rock

Here is an overlooked hard rock band that delivers some bouncy grooves. The Godz debut self-titled release is for sure one that should have gotten people in the mood to rock, but they didn't. From the opening bounce rocker "Go Away," the cruising power jam "Gotta Keep A Runnin," and the Aerosmith styled blues number "Baby I Love You" bring a lot to the table. However, this is an album that you throw up in the air and question, why you didn't know about it until now. This is one of those 70s albums that hardcore rock fans probably owned and stuck at the bottom of the collection. The Godz are one band that need to have this record dusted off.

Goo Goo Dolls – Jed (Metal Blade - 1989) Punk Rock

When most people think the Goo Goo Dolls, you usually think of that modern rock band from the 90s that had great pop gems like "Iris," "Name" and "Black Balloon." What many people don't realize is that this band from the Buffalo NY area has been around since the mid-80s and playing a punk rock style in a similar vein to Husker Du and The Replacements. My first taste of the Goo Goo Dolls was with *Jed* during my college years. They were a band with a combination of fast riffs, songs clocking under three minutes and showing some of the melodic parts that would become a part of their musical framework when they moved into the 90s. Songs like "Up Yours" were straight up punk rock while "Out Of Sight" and "No Way Out" were quicker/melodic punk rock numbers. Also, their version of the Rolling Stones "Gimmie Shelter" is in perfect punk fashion. Of course, it would not be until 1995 when the Goo Goo Dolls became one of the most prominent modern rock acts of the period. *Jed* is one of the early stepping stones of a band on its way to bigger-and-better things during the grunge/modern rock 90s.

Gothic Slam – Just A Face In The Crowd (Epic - 1989) Thrash Metal

The 80s was not just about new wave and glam metal. There was another wave of bands known for thrash metal. Of course, the godfathers of the genre were Metallica, Megadeth, Slayer, and Anthrax, but by the late 80s, other bands were trying to make a claim to be the 5th band on that list. So major labels were linking up with groups from all over the world looking for that one band that could rise to the top. Gothic Slam was one of those bands that made it to the dance (or mosh pit). In 1989, they hooked up with Epic records and the result was *Just A Face In The Crowd*. The album is full of soaring guitar solos, aggressive, high pitched-vocals and plenty of headbanging material. Songs like "Who Died And Made You God," the political edged "Battered Youth" and the pit enticing Thin Lizzy cover "Thunder And Lightning," complete with group chorus chants place the band in similar territory with Anthrax within the genre. It is surprising that Gothic Slam did not get more attention. Then again, the competition was very high at the time, and they were trying to garner the same spots Exodus, Overkill and Testament were trying to claim. If you were a fan of thrash metal and not familiar with this band, you need to check out what you missed.

H-I

Harvey Danger – King James Version (Sire - 2000) Alternative Rock

Let's face facts, Harvey Danger is known for one song and one song only, the iconic "Flagpole Sitta." It's unfortunate that this band did not have more success after that song. Which makes figuring out why *King James Version*, the band's 2nd album was pretty much ignored such a mystery. Lyrically and musically, they could be classified as a "poor man's Weezer," and that's not actually a bad thing. Listen to "Sad Sweetheart Of The Rodeo," "Meetings With Remarkable Men – Show Me the Hero" and "Theme From (Carjack City)" to get a true idea of what this band is all about. Based on various stories, *King James Version* was doomed from the start; label issues, tour issues and lead single "Sad Sweetheart Of The Rodeo" was not well received by radio or MTV. The band would only last a few more years before calling it quits.

Hawthorne Heights – Zero (Red - 2012) Alternative Rock

Hawthorne Heights have been classified as everything from emo, post-hardcore and even pop punk in their career. So, genre-hopping aside, this was one band that had both a combination of underdog success and a series of misfortunes over the same period. In 2012, the group would release *Zero*, an album that took the best elements of their sound and progressed. One of the real highlights of the band's music is vocalist and primary songwriter JT Woodruff and his way to make his lyrics relate to the listener. Nine years after their Victory debut, *The Silence In Black And White* and the musical stylings matured but the lyrical content still relates. One of the songs that flat out showcased the best of the band is the heavy "Taken

By The Dark," which brings back some of those missed screamo/hardcore stylings displayed on earlier albums. The band had moved away from screaming after guitarist Casey Calvert died in 2007. Other songs like pop punk sounds of "Memories And Misery" and the moody hard rock stomp of "Darkside" show a band that can play across the musical spectrum. Maligned by the many labels that had been placed on them, Hawthorne Heights never reached the accolades they deserved, derailing the band before reaching their peak. *Zero* is one of the band's best releases, but the decline was already in place for a group that had so much promise.

Heaven & Earth – Dig (Quatro Valley - 2013) Hard Rock

One of the most original bands to come along in the late 60s, early 70s was Deep Purple. Their blend of hard rock, psychedelic and at times prog rock was often imitated but never quite reached the depths of the great Deep Purple. Then there is a band like Heaven & Earth, who in 2013 release *Dig* and suddenly, we have a group that gets it. The fantastic keyboard/organ sounds alone stand out on this release, but with powerful vocals and terrific guitar work, *Dig* is a gem that sounds like it could have been released in the 70s. Songs like the melodic and psych-tinged "No Money, No Love" show a band where each member is equal parts of an excellent song. Songs like "Waiting For The End Of The World" and "Victorious" have some moving moments that show a band that fans of various styles could gravitate to. Some tracks display elements of blues rock which is unique. While pretty much set on an underground fanbase, Heaven & Earth is a band to search for. If you are a fan of Deep Purple, Rainbow and Black Country Communion, you must listen to this almost unknown gem.

Helmet – Betty (Interscope - 1994) Hard Rock

When the Nirvana wave rolled in, it wasn't wrong for people searching for "The Next Nirvana." In 1992, Helmet released *Meantime*. An album that rode a wave with powerful groove riffs that have influenced the likes of Deftones, Linkin Park, Staind, Godsmack and others that followed them. The hype was already there for the next release, and in 1994 *Betty* was released. Not as heavy and ballistic as Meantime, Page Hamilton and company focused more on other styles like jazz and blues weaved into their noise rock/metal sound. Standout tracks like "Milquetoast," "Wilma's Rainbow" and "Vaccination" have many trademarks of much of the same music that you hear from nu-metal and even post-hardcore bands. Despite *Betty* being the band's highest charting disc, it's never gotten much traction past that. Which would happen when fans are looking for another *Meantime*, and the group threw a pretty good curveball that nobody caught.

The High Speed Scene – S/T (Interscope - 2005) Power Pop

One for the unknown files. The High Speed Scene is a California band that plays a massive brand of Power Pop. The influences will remind you of Weezer and Harvey Danger with more of a pop, maybe even an 80s new wave flavor (minus the keyboards). One of the major tracks is "The I Roc Z Song," which is surprising that this song was not an instant smash on radio or MTV. Not to mention the lyrical references of Eddie Van Halen, Oakleys and Taco Bell in the song. Other tracks like "Crazy Star" and "For The Kids" are more of the same from a band that pretty much came and went without much attention. This is a band that needs to be pulled from the rock they got placed under, and a few extra spins are required.

HSAS – Through The Fire (Geffen - 1984) Hard Rock

Plenty of "supergroups" have forged over rock's history. One that doesn't quite get their due is HSAS, comprised of Sammy Hagar on vocals, Neil Schon on guitar, Kenny Aaronson on bass and Michael Shrieve on drums. While we know Hagar has been very successful as both a solo artist and his work with Montrose, Van Halen and Chickenfoot and Schon being a major component to Journey as well as Santana's band, this should have been a slam dunk. Add Aaronson, who is a very accomplished bassist working with numerous artists including Rick Derringer and Shrieve was a drummer for Santana, only added to what made for an ultimate rock band. *Through The Fire* was recorded live and parts of the album are edited removing the crowd. Starting with the driving hard rocker "Top Of The Rock," which was the main radio track, HSAS was just getting started. Other tracks like the heavy power ballad "He Will Understand" and the bluesy rocker "My Home Town" show a band that sounded like they had been together for a decade. *Through The Fire* was more of a side project and never meant to materialize into anything significant. With Schon still with Journey and Hagar's successful solo career and eventual move to singing for Van Halen, one could understand why. This is one album in Hagar's incredible career that does not get a lot of love outside of fans of his collection. Through the Fire is an album that deserved to be way more significant than it was.

I, Omega – Transients (Bullet Tooth - 2014) Progressive Metal

A progressive metal band from Kentucky, I, Omega is a band that was a blip on the radar for most. When they released *Transients* in 2014, they were a band that fired on all cylinders and a prog band that knew how to bring the metal. With dual guitars that could stand with any big names and a vocalist that could go melodic or screamo depending on what the song needed, and everything locked in perfectly. One of the songs that is a must listen is "Half Way Home," which reminded me slightly of something Coheed & Cambria would do if they decided to go in a more metal direction. Other tracks like the guitar clinic noodling of "Shaking Hands With Sinatra" and the epic sounding "En Longa Somnum (Act. III)", which clocks in at a little over 7 minutes. I, Omega was a band that had some promise and could have been the next prog metal band that could take it to the next level. Sadly, the group has broken up so that will probably not become a reality. That's too bad because despite not really being on a significant level, they were incredibly talented.

Icarus Witch – Rise (Cleopatra - 2012) Hard Rock

As hard rock and heavy metal have changed over the years, one style that always seemed to be the accurate representation of the genre was power metal. The combination of dual guitars, keyboards, soaring vocals, and imaginative lyrics were still the common threads, and artists like Helloween and Manowar seem to put this into the forefront in the 80s. There have been plenty of bands that continue to play this style, mostly in Europe but there is one band in 2012 from the US that put together a brilliant album. They are none other than Icarus Witch. This Pittsburgh band had been around since the early 2000's and had been carving a pretty good underground path over the years. With *Rise*, Icarus Witch had laid down a masterpiece. All the components were locked in, and this band had everything going in their favor. Songs like "(We Are) The New Revolution," the title track and "Break The Cycle" show a band that can stand toe to toe with the giants of the genre. The big problem is that this album failed to break down any barriers as radio passed on most of these style bands a long time ago. Despite the fantastic effort, Icarus Witch continued down its underground path, which we are sure is appreciated by their core audience. Another note, former vocalist Christopher Shaner can flat out wail and is very underrated in our opinion. He has a voice that everyone needs to hear. Icarus Witch is still putting out new music as of this review.

Incubus – S.C.I.E.N.C.E. (Epic - 1997) Hard Rock

Before Incubus became a very successful heavy alternative rock band putting out amazing songs like "Drive" and "Wish You Were Here," they were a combination of nu-metal, rap, and funk metal. Think Red Hot Chili Peppers influenced by Pantera and a DJ in the background. In a world where Korn, Limp Bizkit, and Deftones were taking heavy music into a different direction, Incubus was on board and taking it a step further. That's what makes *S.C.I.E.N.C.E.* a great listen and an album that needs to be either re-listened or discovered by fans that missed out on the band's work before 1999. Their combination of power, funk, percussion and adding scratches and mixes into hard rock style tracks was art. This was music for people that wanted to groove or jump in the mosh pit. "New Skin" is the best example of what Incubus best represented. They put within the guitar, bass and drums a layer of additional percussion in bongos, a DJ mix for additional texture and the vocals of Brandon Boyd, who could be a cross between Anthony Kiedis and Jonathan Davis but more melodic than the two. Other tracks like "Glass," "Vitamin" and "A Certain Shade Of Green" also capture this interesting musical ride both vocally and instrumentally. Incubus would move on to tighter song structures (and radio-friendly tracks) with 1999's *Make Yourself*, but if you listen, you can still hear sounds that made Incubus one of the few bands that could meld funk and metal.

Information Society – Don't Be Afraid (Cleopatra - 1997) Industrial Rock

In the late 80s, new wave/synthpop band Information Society had a huge hit with "What's on Your Mind (Pure Energy)." Yet, they never really got much of a reception when the 90s came outside of some dance club hits. When the music scene took a complete 360 on everyone with the explosion of grunge and alternative music in general, there were a few bands that attempted to blend in. Some of those bands found their way into industrial music, such as artists like Nine Inch Nails, Ministry and Marilyn Manson. Those bands and others began to give that style of music an audience. I mean, it's aggressive music with synths that make you want to mosh and groove in the pit. One band that decided to head in that direction were the Minnesota crew in Information Society, who in 1997 released *Don't Be Afraid*. Most fans of the band by this time probably thought the band had retired but for those who did stick around saw quite a transformation. Musically, it's very dark, and any kind of pop stylings are a distant memory. The sound is somewhere between Depeche Mode meets Orgy and is really a change that the band transitioned to very well. Some of the tracks that standout includes the melodic chaos of "On The Outside," the spontaneous soundscape of "Closing In" and a version of "Are Friends Electric" written by new wave alum Gary Numan. Most of the songs clock in over the six-minute mark, so probably more for the alternative club circuit than radio singles. Despite putting together an exciting release, the album failed to garner much attention. Probably a combination of being an industrial band near the bottom of the rung and just another 80s band not being taken seriously after a musical direction change. We recently found out that the band is still alive and well and have released quite a few albums. If you are looking to catch up, *Don't Be Afraid* will be a treat.

INXS – Full Moon Dirty Hearts (Atlantic - 1993) Alternative Rock

By 1987, INXS was one of the biggest acts in the US with *Kick* being their biggest selling album at that time. The band would begin to see a decline, but still able to be a platinum-selling artist with post- *Kick* releases. *Full Moon, Dirty Hearts* seems to be a release that sticks out as the beginning of the band's downward spiral. Compared to other releases, it has a bit of a darker vibe. Perhaps they were a band noticing the changes of the time with grunge and 90s alternative rock? That does not mean that their songs were lacking any kind of strength. Listening to tracks like "Make Your Peace," "Time" and "Cut Your Roses Down" still contain the trademark musical swagger of their previous albums. However, it does not seem that radio picked up this record. Which would also mean that fans of the bands 80s collection had moved on as well. While we could understand how "hair bands" and 70s artists faded off by 1993, it's a wonder how INXS sort of fell off at this point. Can we blame the Spin Doctors?

J-K

Jim Santora with Jesse James Dupree of Jackyl (photo by Jennifer Hickman)

Jackyl – Best In Show (Mighty Loud - 2012) Hard Rock

For most people, they only know Jackyl from their 1992 single "The Lumberjack," featuring the chainsaw solo courtesy of vocalist Jesse James Dupree. They came in at the end of the glam era and the beginning of the grunge era. There were several southern style bands like The Black Crowes, Collective Soul, Raging Slab, Drivin N Cryin and Brother Cane all trying to stand out in the early 90s. Jackyl was the loudest of the bunch, a combination of AC/DC meets southern rock. By 2012, Jackyl was still making noise with *Best In Show*, twelve tracks full of southern bounce, infectious grooves and filled with songs of sex, women and the road. Some of the standout tracks are the heavy southern blues of "Favorite Sin," the girl on the pole swinging "Encore" and the head bouncing grooves of "Screwdriver." Jesse and company even spin their own take of "Cover Of Rolling Stone" and Run D.M.C.'s "It's Tricky." Overall, it's a straight-up rock record with some fantastic songs that seriously got overlooked by the masses.

Jeffrey Gaines – S/T (Chrysalis - 1992) Rock

A solo performer whose style ranged from rock to singer-songwriter genres alike, Jeffrey Gaines got his break with his self-titled debut in 1992. Gaines was years ahead of other singer-songwriters with a rock sound like Edwin McCain and Hootie & The Blowfish. So, it's not surprising that this album did not fare well at a time when grunge was pretty much dominating the music scene. Lead single "Hero In Me" is a very underrated acoustic driven rock song. Gaines is very talented both vocally and lyrically. Other songs like "Fear" have a dose of John Cougar Mellencamp stylings thrown in and closing track "Headmasters Of Mine" may have you thinking about your childhood. Gaines would continue recording into the 2000's, and his cover of Peter Gabriel's "In Your Eyes" became a minor hit, years after its debut. If you are new to Jeffrey Gaines, you need to start at the beginning.

Judas Priest – Sad Wings Of Destiny (Gull - 1976) Metal

While it would still be a few more years before Judas Priest would become household names in Metal with songs like "Living After Midnight" and "Breaking The Law." In 1976, they were more of a band that had that Led Zeppelin meets Black Sabbath approach. While those two bands would become staples for many hard rock and metal bands to follow, Judas Priest had another element that was truly their own. On *Sad Wings Of Destiny*, they had the sonic vocals of Rob Halford, who shows early on that he is a voice that everyone will remember. In their bag of tricks is the two-guitar attack of Glenn Tipton and K.K. Downing. *Sad Wings Of Destiny* is also an album that is not predictable as its tracks contain a collection of various song structures, even stretching to a prog element in a few. Just listen to "Victim Of Changes," "The Ripper" and "Tyrant" to get the general flow of this album. Again, it would be a few more years until *Hell Bent For Leather* would catapult Judas Priest into another level among the biggest names in hard rock/metal. That being said, *Sad Wings Of Destiny* is indeed an album that shows the band utilizing everything in their bag of tricks as they would march through the 70s eventually becoming one of the most recognized group's in the world.

Juliana Hatfield – Only Everything (Atlantic - 1995) Alternative Rock

In the 80s, Hatfield was the vocalist and bassist for Blake Babies, who garnered some attention on college radio. When that band broke up, Juliana set out on her own, and by 1993, her *Become What You Are* album was praised, and songs like "My Sister" and "Spin The Bottle" were staples on modern rock radio and MTV. In 1995, she released *Only Everything*. It seemed like this record came late to the grunge party and many of the songs were heavier in tone and had no problem with increasing the distortion. Despite the change in direction, everything fits. Hatfield has great vocals, and *Only Everything* proved that she could rock out. Stand out tracks include "Universal Heart-Beat," the acoustic-driven "Hang Down from Heaven" and the full-on rocker "What A Life." Hatfield would continue to put out material, some that would fall as underrated albums for sure, but Only Everything was apparently one that got pushed aside.

Kansas – Masque (Kirshner-1975) Progressive Rock

Masque was the third album released from Kansas. We are still an album away from "Carry On Wayward Son," but this might be the best work from Kansas before their string of multi-platinum releases. On *Masque*, Kansas is a band that shows off stellar musicianship, great vocal harmonies and their biggest staple, the work of Robby Steinhardt on violin. The album managed to crack the Top 100 in the album charts but the first single, "It Takes A Woman's Love (To Make A Man)" failed to crack radio. The one track that shows the band at their highest potential on this record is "Icarus – Borne On Wings Of Steel." This is one song that should have been up amongst some of the best prog rock tracks of the time. Sadly, *Masque* is one of those hidden treasures in the Kansas catalog. If someone was ever getting into prog rock, obviously Yes and Rush would be solid choices, but *Masque* should be part of a person's musical journey.

Kelly Clarkson – My December (RCA - 2007) Pop Rock

Now there are going to be people reading this review and merely going what the?!?!? Well, before you start screaming, one needs to get their hands on *My December*, the third album released by the first star of *American Idol*. This album is Kelly going more rock and showing she is not a pop diva, and she pulls this off. Beginning with the first single "Never Again," a dark song and Clarkson shows plenty of attitude and anger to go with her melodic voice. Other songs like the bluesy number "Dirty Little Secret" and the modern rock sounding "Hole" show a different side of Clarkson. The rest of the album contains more acoustic driven tracks and of course enough pop synths to keep things honest. After all, Kelly needs to keep that Top 40 shine. Over the years, Clarkson has continued to add more rock songs to her albums. Clarkson writes most of the material but does get some co-writers in Chantal Kreviazuk and Our Lady Peace's Raine Maida on the track "One Minute." Sometimes, you need to open the blinders a little bit more to see where pop artists want to rock, and *My December* is one of those other pieces of the musical landscape that you should see.

Kevn Kinney of Drivin N Cryin (photo courtesy of the artist)

Kevn Kinney – Macdougal Blues (Island - 1990) Folk Rock

While Drivin N Cryin is one of the most underrated and overlooked bands ever. What people end up missing is the unique storytelling lyrics of frontman Kevn Kinney. While early DNC songs fell somewhere between folk rock, southern rock, hard rock, and even country, Kinney was always looking to step out on his own with his more folk style songs. In 1990, he would release *Macdougal Blues*, which in many ways, is an acoustic Drivin N Cryin album with Kinney's name on it (DNC would act as the backing band on most of the tracks). Here is where Kinney's lyrics take shape, and you are on the attention of every word. Songs about traveling folk singers, the dark side of comedians, eccentric women living above supermarkets and just wanting to get away from it all, it's all on this album. Standout tracks include "Gotta Get Outta Here," "Lost And Found" and "Heard

The Laughter Ending" are just a part of the picture. Kinney's solo work probably gets even more overlooked than DNC's, which would eventually take off when the band released *Fly Me Courageous* in 1991.

Killer Dwarfs – Dirty Weapons (Epic - 1990) Hard Rock

Killer Dwarfs were a hard-rocking Canadian band that had more in common with straight-up hard rock bands than the glam bands of the 80s. Of course, the territory they are in kind of lumped them into the mix. They did have sort of a Ramones approach as all the members of the band had the last name of Dwarf, and their videos always tried to show their humorous side. They had a breakthrough in Canada with *Stand Tall*, paving the way in 1988 for Big Deal. When *Dirty Weapons* was released in 1990, the stage was set for Killer Dwarfs to make a name for themselves. This album is undoubtedly the heaviest of their releases, with "Comin Through" and the title track showing more metallic muscle than in the past. That did not mean, they did not have a soft side. After all, this is the period of the power ballad, and they lay their emotions down with "Doesn't Matter." Despite their efforts, they were still just an under the radar band in the US and eventually would disband in the 1990's. They still have a hardcore fanbase, and the band has been on the road touring and releasing music. Killer Dwarfs are still fighting the fight.

Killer Dwarfs (photo courtesy of the artist)

King's X – Ear Candy (Atlantic - 1996) Hard Rock

Let's forget about albums for a second. King's X might be the most underrated and underappreciated band of all-time. How they have never been a huge arena rock act baffle many. In the meantime, King's X continues to tour and have a very loyal and dedicated fan base. After King's X moved out of the 80s and got lumped into the hair band era, they continued to march on in the 90s. While the Warrant's and Ratt's of the world were pushed aside by the likes of Alice In Chains, Nirvana and Pearl Jam, there was King's X still in the mix. While obviously not as big as the other bands mentioned, they rocked with *Dogman* in 1994, got an opportunity to play Woodstock and were climbing the ladder. So, in 1996, the trio of Dug Pinnick, Ty Tabor, and Jerry Gaskill release *Ear Candy*, a disc full of melodic heavy rockers and lighter driven songs that might capture all the best elements of the band in one album. Some of the songs that standout is the ballad "A Box," featuring Glen Phillips of Toad the Wet Sprocket, the melodic hard rock opener "The Train" and what should have been a radio hit in "Mississippi Moon." It's really one of those records where despite having what could have been four or five radio songs, this album only made it to #102 on the charts. They could have been a contender, and this record instead was the last Atlantic release. Not a hidden gem but a classic that never was.

Jim Santora with King's X (photo by Jennifer Hickman)

Kiss – Music From The Elder (Casablanca - 1981) Classic Rock

Throughout the career of Kiss, they have always continued to face criticism. From starting out as an over the top band from New York City, at the height of their worldwide success and even 40+ years later still touring and finally members of the Rock N Roll Hall of Fame. In the late 70s, the wheels were starting to fall off for the band, particularly after *Love Gun* in 1978. So, the band releases solo albums, then they go disco. Finally, they do what any other band would do next, a movie soundtrack. What kind of suicide is that? Anyone remember when Queen did the *Flash Gordon* soundtrack? The band embarks on a movie soundtrack for *The Elder*, a movie that has never seen the light of day. While that remains a mystery, the music is for sure something different than anything Kiss ever did in their career. Somewhere in their mix is elements of Pink Floyd and Progressive Rock styles. There is nothing close to the makeup-wearing, platform shoe wearing, fire-breathing band that made them a household name. While fans were shunning this album, some classics got overlooked in songs like "The Oath," "A World Without Heroes" and "Only You." What this shows is a band that was not afraid to come out of their comfort zone and does a complete about-face. It also showed a group that was more than just three-chord rock. This album has some excellent musicianship and vocal harmonies that were not seen in the band's previous album catalog. Over the years, even the band itself have pushed this album aside. If anything, *The Elder* shows a group that tried to step out of the box and grow and did not look at what it may cost. Good news for Kiss was that they made a very successful comeback through the 80s and onward, after this release.

The Knack – Serious Fun (1991 – Capitol) Classic Rock

Let's get serious. Back in the late 70s, there was no song bigger than The Knack's "My Sharona." In fact, it is still receiving airplay, so I am sure those checks are still rolling in for the band. After that, there was not much to talk about regarding the band. A true one hit wonder and a band that most people are sure drifted off somewhere when the 80s turned. You would be wrong again. The Knack was still alive and kicking into the early 90s. That's where we find *Serious Fun* and the band putting out an album full of power pop rock gems. Songs like the rocker "River Of Sighs," the bubblegum pop of "Rocket O Love" and the ballad "One Day At A Time" show the band in a variety of styles. Overall a great listen. The downfall here for The Knack is that it's the 90s, and the musical landscape was changing. Which means that bands like The Knack and others put out albums full of catchy songs that were basically ignored. If you are a fan of power pop and classic 70s, then give this one a listen.

The Knack (photo courtesy of the band)

Kopek – White Collar Lies (Religion - 2011) Modern Rock

Kopek is a three-piece from Ireland that takes parts of various genres to put together one of the best albums that most people have no idea even existed. The Kopek sound is equal parts classic rock, grunge, and punk. This combination could be a reason the band managed to get radio play on both modern and hard rock radio. *White Collar Lies* is led by the classic opener "Love Is Dead" and is filled with amazing tracks front to back. Other standouts include the heavier "Cocaine Chest Pains" and the hard rock melodic cruiser "Fever." It's still a surprise that Kopek never really made it huge on the charts in the US. Just another example of a band with all the talent that gets ignored. The group would release Rise a few years later, but it also failed to do much for the band.

Jim Santora with Kopek (photo by Jennifer Hickman)

Kyuss – …And The Circus Leaves Town (Elektra - 1995) Stoner Rock

Kyuss is probably one of the bands at the front of the line when talking about the stoner rock genre. However, by the time …*And The Circus Leaves Town* was released in 1995, the band would be pretty much broken up. This album in some sort of way failed to generate a lot of steam. First, this is a bottom-heavy album that will rattle your skull. Songs like "Hurricane," "One Inch Man" and "El Rodeo" set the tone for one lo-fi heavy doom trip of an album. It was produced by Chris Goss of Masters of Reality fame and would go on to produce many records from Queens of The Stone Age, which Kyuss guitarist Josh Homme leads and had been successful. If only Kyuss had stuck it out a little longer, they could have been a contender. One could say if not for Kyuss, we may not have seen bands like QOTSA, Fu Manchu and Clutch continue to pave the way through the 90s.

L-M

L7 – Hungry For Stink (Slash – 1994) Grunge Rock

L7 is probably the first in a series of all-female groups in the early 90s that were super heavy. While the 80s were pushing out Go-Go's and Bangles in the early part of the decade, and artists like Vixen, Hellion and Girlschool were the hard rock side of the spectrum, there was this underground band known as L7. *Hungry For Stink* is a follow-up to their best album, 1992's *Bricks Are Heavy*. L7 was not a band that was going to play it down the middle nor were they going to give you pretty power ballads. They were a loud band that drew a fine line between punk and metal. They often get lumped into the grunge genre, but they usually were more metal than their counterparts. While *Hungry For Stink* is sort of an album that gets lost from the band, they have some noteworthy songs including the lead single "Andres," the Runaway's inspired "Can I Run" and the moody "Stuck Here Again." L7 is another band that gets overshadowed by their grunge contemporaries. It could be very well that they were a group of women rocking in a man's world, but they were so much more and could blow plenty of bands out in the process. *Hungry For Stink* is proof of that.

The Leaving Trains – F*** (SST - 1987) Punk Rock

I didn't really get a full dose of understanding punk rock until college. One of those first bands I gravitated to was a California group known as The Leaving Trains. In 1987, they released *F****, which is 14 songs of punk/indie rock gold. The Leaving Trains were never a household name, and if ever mentioned, it was that vocalist Falling James Moreland was married to Courtney Love in the late 80s. Aside from that, James and the band had pretty much found a home on college radio and on the SST label, that brought us Husker Du, Meat Puppets, Dinosaur Jr and Black Flag to name a few. The Leaving Trains never disappoint on this release as they weave back and forth into a Punk vs. Indie Rock wave throughout. Standout tracks include "Walking With You," "What Cissy Said" and "27 Days". *F**** showed a lot of promise for the band, but when the 90s started the shift towards grunge and alternative rock, The Leaving Trains got left behind and eventually would disband in 2001.

Led Zeppelin – Presence (Swan Song - 1976) Hard Rock

Probably the most overlooked album in the Led Zeppelin catalog, Led Zeppelin's *Presence* was just another musical adventure in creativity. Was there really anything this heavy blues-rock band couldn't do? One of the biggest detractors for *Presence* was the fact that during the same time, the group also had the live concert movie *"The Song Remains The Same,"* which could be a reason several of the songs on this album do not get as recognized as some of their other classics. Listening to the opening track "Achilles Last Stand" which clocks in at over 10 minutes is everything you imagine from Led Zeppelin; the guitar work of Jimmy Page, the soaring vocal work of Robert Plant and the rhythm section of John Paul Jones and John Bonham make this one of the most talented and creative bands on the planet. Other tracks that standout includes the sonic blues rocker "Nobody's Fault But Mine" and "Tea For One," which is another song hovering around the 10 minutes mark. Led Zeppelin is one of the most recognized and influential bands ever, yet even they have their one album that kind of gets pushed a little to the back. Time to let the *Presence* be known again.

Legs Diamond – A Diamond Is A Hard Rock (Mercury - 1977) Hard Rock

Legs Diamond is a Los Angeles, hard rock band that has a Deep Purple feel. On their second release, the group weaves a rocking web that is full of impressive vocals, hard rock riffs, and keyboards that could put this band more in the vein of bands like Angel. Musically, one could see how many of the 80s bands could have grasped some influences from Legs Diamond. Standout tracks include "Woman," "Jailbait," and the title track. Their lo-fi hard rock sound mixed at times with some prog rock stylings (again, keyboards) keep this disc interesting. At times, vocalist Rick Sanford had similarities to Judas Priest's Rob Halford, and one needs to wonder why Legs Diamond is not more of a household name. Very underrated vocalist and band in general.

The Lemonheads – Come On Feel The Lemonheads (Atlantic - 1993) Alternative Rock

The Lemonheads are a New England band lead by Evan Dando. Starting their career in the mid/late 80s, they were an indie punk band. Songs were fast and ranging in the 2-minute mark, but you could tell that Dando was a talented songwriter. In 1992, Lemonheads would release It's A Shame About Ray, which was the bands breakthrough. Led by their cover of Simon and Garfunkel's "Mrs. Robinson." By the time *Come On Feel The Lemonheads* was released in 1993, it should have taken the band to even greater heights. The lead single "Into Your Arms" is still a classic in my opinion. Great songwriting, melodic, everything fits musically. The song was top of the alternative charts but should have been huge beyond that. Other tracks like "The Great Big No" sound like they came off a Smithereens record but stand out regardless. Meanwhile, "Style" still shows a band that hasn't lost the punk edge. Despite all of this, the record fell on deaf ears by many and sadly, the only thing people remember from this band is a song that they did as a cover.

Life Of Agony – Broken Valley (Epic - 2005) Metal

Talk about one band that was misclassified, which could be a significant reason why Life Of Agony was not more of a force in the rock world in the 1990's. They were a band from Brooklyn, New York and rubbed shoulders with many of the bands from the NY Hardcore scene. They had a series of records in the 90s that helped them gain a fan base, but nothing more than a blip on the radar. Also, they were often classified more as metal than hard rock. They could have been huge if they were classified with the grunge movement that made its way to music history. The band would sort of implode in the late 90s, then make its comeback with 2005's *Broken Valley*. Life of Agony shows no signs of a layoff as they display themselves as a tremendous loud band with great vocals led by Keith (now Mina) Caputo. The album kicks off with "Love To Let You Down" which is a heavy and quick paced number showcasing some of their hardcore roots. Other songs like "Last Cigarette" have a Stone Temple Pilots quality while "Junk Sick" has an Alice In Chains vibe until you get to the vocals, where there is no mistaking Caputo's melodic qualities. This album ended up being a commercial failure by Epic's standards but remains as the highest charting album in Life Of Agony's history.

Lillian Axe – XI: The Days Before Tomorrow (CME - 2012) Hard Rock

The late 80s early 90s pretty much was doomsday for the hair/glam bands. One of those casualties was Lillian Axe, a group that had plenty of promise but when the 90s rolled through, groups like Lillian Axe got run over. Down but not out, Lillian Axe has continued to move forward, and in

2012, they released their eleventh album *The Days Before Tomorrow*. Long gone from the hair band 80s, Lillian Axe fires on all cylinders with this album as the band go more into a power metal direction. Dual guitars and soaring, melodic vocals are true standouts throughout this record. Tracks like "Death Comes Tomorrow," "Caged In" and "Babylon" show a band that has weathered the storm and are still standing. Lillian Axe is still not a household name but *The Days Before Tomorrow* is a great album that needs to be discovered.

Lillian Axe (photo courtesy of band)

Living Colour – Stain (Epic - 1993) Hard Rock

When people have conversations about alternative metal and where it traces back to, and you're not mentioning Living Colour, then you have no idea what you're talking about. Here was a band that could play hard rock/metal, funk rock and pretty much anything else they wanted to do. Now they have one huge song in "Cult Of Personality," which today still sounds as relevant as it did 30 years ago. While the *Vivid* album set the tone, the second album *Time's Up* earned them a Grammy award. In 1993, the band would return with *Stain*, an album that displayed the band at their heaviest but not losing any of the funk or experimental style of their previous releases. First, we need to state that guitarist Vernon Reid may be on the list of underrated and overlooked players. Second, Corey Glover is an amazing vocalist who also gets overlooked. Songs like the heavy rocker "Leave It Alone" show off the talents of a band that can be as heavy as they want to be, while the song "Bi" shows off the funky rock side of the band. Meanwhile, "Mind Your Own Business" is a song showing a punk/thrash metal side. With Living Colour you get a bag of tricks and then some. *Stain* sort of derailed a bit amongst the alternative/grunge scene. By 1995, the band would break up for a time before regrouping. This is an album that needs to get a definite re-listen.

Lizzy Borden – Visual Lies (Metal Blade - 1987) Hard Rock

One of the most under the radar bands of the Hard Rock 80s was Lizzy Borden. While other groups on the Sunset Strip were getting picked up by the major labels, it was Lizzy Borden carrying the metal torch and some indie cred on Metal Blade. In 1987, they released *Visual Lies*, and perhaps if they were on one of the majors, they could have been more of a household name in the late 80s. With songs like the power metal anthem "Me Against The World," it's hard to argue the talent. Other standout tracks include "Outcast" and "Eyes Of A Stranger." While the hair bands of the day were upbeat and always having a party, Lizzy Borden's lyrics were darker, and the music was raw and lacked the polish, which is not a bad thing. Of course, this was a band that did not catch the attention of the masses outside of their core fanbase. Which was unfortunate for a group that could stand with any of the top bands of the 80s.

Local H – Pack Up The Cats (UMG - 1998) Alternative Rock

The 90s for the sake of argument was a great time for rock. Everyone was different. Or the same, but different. Yes, confusing times indeed. Which brings us to Local H. With their *As Good as Dead* album spawning the awesome sounding "Bound To The Floor," Local H was destined to become a super band. Hard rocking sound with a post-Nirvanish tone. How could they not be great? Oh, did we mention that it's around this time, the two-man band became a thing? Before the White Stripes, Black Keys and Royal Blood, there was Local H. In 1998, *Pack Up The Cats* is released. A full-throttle hard rocking grunge record. The band has a great tone in their music and songs like the sonic soundings of "What Can I Tell You," the cowbell/fuzz infusion of "Cool Magnet" or the headbanging opener of "Oh Yeah (All Right)." Despite the infectious sounding tracks, *Pack Up The Cats* failed to gain the momentum of the previous release. Perhaps for some, they sounded too much like Nirvana. What those people missed is what Local H did with their sound that Nirvana had not.

The Loud Family – Interbabe Concern (Alias - 1996) Alternative Rock

If there is one single person that could be the most underrated and over-looked in this book, it's Scott Miller. Beginning with Game Theory, he amassed a run of albums in the 80s that only made that band a college staple when they should have been riding a wave with other alternative bands like R.E.M. Once that group disbanded, Miller began work on the next phase and formed The Loud Family. This band had a little more grit than Game Theory, but Scott was an intriguing songwriter and was not afraid to show his quirky and prog sides in songs. A few albums in, The Loud Family released *Interbabe Concern* in 1996. Out of all the bands work in the 90s, this release may be the closest to some of Miller's best work with Game Theory. The album is full of lyrical gems and numerous sound effects to go along with their version of alternative power pop. Some of the standout tracks include "Don't Respond She Can Tell," "Sodium Laureth Sulfate" and "Top Dollar Survivalist Hardware." Listening to *Interbabe Concern* is for headphones only. It is unfortunate that this was another release that was ignored. Miller would continue to do work with The Loud Family and eventually pack up in 2006. Miller was a true over-looked master of his craft who passed away too soon in 2013.

Loudness – Thunder In The East (Atco - 1985) Hard Rock

I've always wondered how American artists like Cheap Trick and Dokken, for example, are huge (Beatle-esque) in Japan, yet the same does not happen to Japanese artists here. One prime example of this is Loudness, a Japanese hard rock/metal band that was the cream of the crop beginning in the early 80s. Loudness was a true metal band that also showed elements of progressive rock at times. Led by the guitar work of Akira Takasaki, even Eddie Van Halen referred to him as the best guitarist in the world. Loudness would arrive in the US, learn English and in 1985, they would release *Thunder In The East*. Loudness would come out at a time where glam metal was starting to become a thing. While bands were going more for the glossy sounds, power ballads, and hairspray, Loudness was playing balls out hard rock. *Thunder In The East* was a grand slam with the anthem rocker "Crazy Nights," the powerful "Heavy Chains" and the thrasher "Get Away." Despite this being a debut in the US, Loudness was already a veteran band that was on top of their game. This album did not disappoint and became the first Japanese album ever to crack the Billboard Top 100 album charts. Despite that accomplishment, Loudness failed to become a sensation with *Thunder In The East*. The band would put out two more albums and eventually kick out vocalist Minoru Niihara in favor of American vocalist Mike Vescera. By the early 90s, Loudness time had run out on dominating hard rock in the US. For people that are not familiar with Loudness, they are one of the most underrated talents musically, and *Thunder In The East* is a must listen.

Love/Hate – Blackout In The Red Room (Columbia - 1990) Hard Rock

Bands like Guns N Roses, L.A. Guns, and Skid Row were coming out in the late 80s and bringing out another whole style of hard rock. They branched away from the glam metal bands and were going more balls to the wall while paying homage to more classic rock n roll. Love/Hate was one of the followers of the same blueprint, and in 1990, they released *Blackout In The Red Room*. Their sound was aggressive, heavy, and, clearly wore their influences on their sleeve. Jizzy Pearl is one of the more underrated vocalists of the time and songs like the title track, "Why Do You Think They Call It Dope" and "Slave Girl" show a band that flat out rocks, can go a little funky when they need to as well as having a slight punk edge. Sadly, Love/Hate would not get much of a run and would become forgotten outside of diehard fans as the band has continued to rock out throughout the 90s and forward.

Magnapop – Hot Boxing (Priority - 1994) Modern Rock

A Modern Rock band out of Atlanta whose members had ties with Michael Stipe and Matthew Sweet is always a plus. Led by vocalist Linda Hopper and guitarist Ruthie Morris, they would release *Hot Boxing* in 1994, produced by modern rock legend Bob Mould. On their second release, they show a very aggressive power pop sound. With catchy hooks and a punk edge throughout, songs like "Lay It Down," "Texas" and "Here It Comes" flat out rock. This is during a time where female-fronted groups and artists were becoming the "in thing." Which may have been the downfall of this release. While *Hot Boxing* is a strong release, other female artists like Juliana Hatfield, PJ Harvey, L7, Veruca Salt and Liz Phair were making their way, it would appear Magnapop got lost outside of a few tracks. In the end, Magnapop got relegated to the college music scene and remained there, only to be heard by few as opposed to the masses they deserved.

Magnapop (photo courtesy of the band)

Mama's Boys – Power And Passion (Zomba - 1985) Hard Rock

During the hard rock 80s, there were plenty of bands that fell so far under the radar, that you mention a band name and people go, "Who?" That's exactly what people say about Ireland's Mama's Boys. Comprised of the McManus brothers, they were a Celtic Rock band before they dropped the traditional instruments and went more for a rock sound. In Europe, the band opened for Thin Lizzy and Hawkwind before going to make a name for themselves in the US. In 1985, they would release *Power And Passion*, an album full of back to basics hard rock songs and on occasion, guitarist Pat McManus would break out a fiddle, which added something interesting to their brand of hard rock. "Needle In The Groove" is the go-to track on this album and the song that if anyone has ever heard of the band may remember or even recognize. Other standout tracks include the melodic "Run" and the title track, which is probably the heaviest song on the album. Mama's Boys are among many of the bands that were part of the NWOBHM (New Wave of British Heavy Metal) but are clearly overshadowed by the top tier bands from that genre both in England and even more so when many of those bands came across the pond. One of many 80s hard rock bands that could not catch a break and *Power And Passion* was an album that was apparently missed by too many ears.

The Mars Volta – De-Loused In The Comatorium (Universal - 2003) Progressive Rock

There was quite a buzz about At the Drive-In when they came out. In my opinion, they were the next level of alternative rock. When they broke up, out of the ashes came The Mars Volta, which was part of a new wave of prog rock in the early 2000's which included Coheed and Cambria. In 2003, the band released *De-Loused In The Comatorium*, which is a conceptual album about a man in a coma after a drug overdose. Anyhow, the album has some great soundscapes throughout and musically is well thought out. Cedric Bixler-Zavala is a very underrated vocalist, and his ability to bob and weave through the musical structures is impressive. Standout tracks include "Drunkship Of Lanterns," "Inertiatic Esp" and "Take The Veil Cerpin Taxt." To a certain extent, you can hear a slight nod to their At the Drive-In days, but it's like the band took that sound and expanded to infinity. Also, to note, The Mars Volta had Flea from Red Hot Chili Peppers handle bass duties, not a poor choice. This band would find more success, Top 10 albums and even a Grammy award in their future, but this is an album that indeed laid the groundwork for an excellent prog album.

Marty Casey and Lovehammers – S/T (Epic - 2006) Alternative Rock

Marty Casey is probably best known as the runner-up from the *Rock Star: INXS* reality show when the band was looking for a lead singer. Some may argue that Casey was the best singer out of the batch. The positive is that he was good enough to become the opening act for INXS while on tour which would lead to a deal with Epic. They then release the self-titled disc with his band the Lovehammers. The music on this record is somewhere between a hard rock version of Soul Asylum, Daughtry and a pinch of Nirvana. It's heavy in moments and melodic throughout. The band has plenty of energy, and the songs all have radio quality from front to back. Standout tracks include the opening hard rocker "Casualty," the melodic modern rocker "Trees" and the grunge rocker "Eyes Can't See." Marty and company would make a small blip on the radar but in the end, they never quite caught on as a band that mattered. They had great songs and sounded awesome, but they sort of got ignored. Casey would eventually be seen fronting a version of L.A. Guns as the years went on as well as doing some more work with the Lovehammers and solo projects. This was an album that clearly got underappreciated and maybe in some circles, unknown.

Mass – New Birth (Retroactive-1985) Hard Rock

By 1985, glam metal was beginning to take over the music landscape. One of the bands trying to make some noise in that arena were Mass. They were a hard rock band from New England that had a combination of metallic sounds, great vocals, and lyrical content. *New Birth* was an album full of promise. This is one album that is not high-gloss in production, and that is an excellent thing. There is something very raw with the sound and makes tracks like "Too Far Gone" and "Watch Her Walk" that much heavier. This was also a band that had a great vocalist in Louie St. August and some very credible guitar work by Gene D'Itira. The stand out tracks are the ballads. "Do You Love Me" is a perfect ballad and should have been the band's calling card, but other than some MTV play, never made it to the next level. Meanwhile, "Day Without You" is another ballad that missed its opportunity and failed to even get noticed. Mass would continue through the 80s, but never really did anything after *New Birth*. While other artists releases I thought were great at the time, they didn't have the same staying power of *New Birth* as one of the best albums of that period of rock. Mass continues to perform and has had several releases in their 30+ year career.

Mass (photo courtesy of the band)

Masters Of Reality – S/T (Def American - 1989) Stoner Rock

If there is a discussion about stoner rock and Masters of Reality is not at the beginning of the topic, then you need to listen to this album. In 1989 (and late 80s in general), the music styles were changing. Hair bands were starting to phase out for groups that were different from what had been going on. One of those bands was Masters of Reality, led by future stoner rock producer Chris Goss, who helped get bands like Queens of the Stone Age on the map. With this debut, Maters of Reality had an element of classic rock, hard rock, prog, and blues that was infectious, and you wanted to listen to more. Standout tracks include "Domino," "John Brown" and "The Candy Song." This is a classic album top to bottom, and it is criminal that this did not become a multimillion seller out the gate. Worth a second listen and if it's the first time you hear about this band, grab your headphones. Oh, and on a side note, the legendary Ginger Baker played drums for Masters of Reality for a bit. You're welcome.

Matthew Sweet – Altered Beast (Zoo - 1993) Alternative Rock

Beating to his own drum, Matthew Sweet's lo-fi power pop sound was almost mind-bending at times. After the successful Girlfriend in 1991, Sweet took his style even further with 1993's *Altered Beast*. An album that despite not containing any of his most popular tracks, could be considered his best work. A heavier record, Sweet was sure to bring the rock beginning with the opening track "Dinosaur Act." Then he followed up with "Devil With The Green Eyes," a song that would sound great as an acoustic but Sweet makes sure the song has some bite. Another song that draws attention is "The Ugly Truth," a massive acoustic number featuring some violin and great vocal harmonies. Come back a few tracks later and "Ugly Truth Rock" is a rockier version of the same song. It's evident that Sweet worried more about writing great songs than writing hits. That's evident here on *Altered Beast*. A fantastic piece of work musically and lyrically which falls right in place between *Girlfriend* and 1995's *100% Fun*.

Medieval – Medieval Kills! (New Renassiance-1987) Metal

One of the most unknown and underrated bands from the 1980's metal scene was a three-piece from Michigan known as Medieval. By the time they released their full-length *Medieval Kills!* on New Renaissance, they had already gotten noticed by having a track on Metal Massacre IV. Part of the CD Compilation series that helped break artists like Metallica, Ratt, Slayer, and Lizzy Borden among others. Unfortunately, once it was released, the break never happened, and the label had shut down. No other offers came calling for the band. Which was a shame because this is one metal treasure that should not be left behind. For one, Medieval is the only band that can somehow cross into what would be considered death rock, Misfits style punk rock and from another direction, grunge rock/metal. Of the 19 tracks, the hate influenced "Blood And Anger", the bottom end chugger "Plague" and power packed "All Knobs To The Right" deliver plenty of punch, while instrumental tracks like "B.F.H." and the cover of the "Peter Gunn Theme" show they didn't need vocals to blow your brains out. It is too bad the band never got a chance to do a significant follow-up from here because we can only imagine what direction they would have gone in the hard rock/metal landscape.

Megadeth – Youthanasia (Capitol - 1994) Metal

During the 1990's, Megadeth had an excellent track record and let's face facts, if not for Metallica, Dave Mustaine and company would have been the top band of the thrash metal scene, no question. *Youthanasia* makes the list primarily because it is wedged between two essential albums, 1992's *Countdown To Extinction* and 1997's *Cryptic Writings*. This album gets overlooked because of its placement. For one, the thrash metal sound that they (along with Metallica, Anthrax, and Slayer) were responsible for, was beginning to find its way out of the band's sound. On the other side, the songs were starting to have more groove and melody, which would pave the way to where their music was going in the late 90s. The tracks that need to be on the listener's list are the metal chugger "Train Of Consequences" and the pseudo-ballad "A Tout Le Monde," which took the band to a different direction than in previous albums. Meanwhile, "Reckoning Day" opens the album and don't worry, the thrash style sounds are not lost. This album did well sales wise, but like every great band, this album is not always sought after today as compared to some of their earlier works. In fact, there are a few that would debate that this was the album that may have caused the somewhat downward spiral of the band heading into the 2000's. Regardless of the reasons, *Youthanasia* is a solid record that should be discussed as being as important as their other releases before it.

Dave Mustaine of Megadeth (photo by Byron Crowley)

Method of Destruction – U.S.A. For M.O.D. (Megaforce – 1987) Hardcore

A spinoff of Stormtroopers of Death, featuring members of Anthrax and Nuclear Assault, vocalist Billy Milano took their brand of thrash/hardcore to another level when he created Methods Of Destruction. The songs are a definite source of early hardcore music. It's loud, aggressive, angry and Milano adds an element of humor in his lyrics. This album does have its share of controversy with some of the topics of the time. *U.S.A. For M.O.D.* may not be for anyone that would take offense. Some of the tracks that flat out destroy are "Get A Real Job," "Let Me Out" and "Dead Man/Most/Captain Crunch." M.O.D. would tone down for upcoming albums like *Surfin M.O.D.* and *Gross Misconduct* as they headed into the 1990's. *U.S.A. For M.O.D.* is one of those rare hardcore music gems that for those into that scene can crank it up again (when nobody is around to offend of course).

Ministry – A Mind Is A Terrible Thing To Taste (Sire - 1989) Industrial Rock

Ministry is considered by many to be the pioneers of Industrial music. Call it rock or metal, it was different and in the 90s there were plenty of bands that embraced it and were successful like Nine Inch Nails. Ministry was initially a new wave synth-pop band. By the late 80s, they elevated their sound to something more aggressive, and loud. We are still two years away from what is their most remarkable record, *Psalm 69* but it's obvious that to build a bridge, you need a piece to tie them together. So that welcome piece is *A Mind Is A Terrible Thing To Taste*. This album is what happens when you combine new wave and thrash/speed metal with a punk rock attitude and further chaos. Sound effects, chants, and other general noises make this not only an album that makes you want to mosh in a pit or throw a chair, but it also makes you sit back and listen through headphones, so you don't miss anything. For some strange trip, this album also had a weird Pink Floyd feel to it. Songs like "Cannibal Song," "Thieves" and "Burning Inside" are essential listens to an album that leads to bigger things for this genre creating group.

Mos Generator – Nomads (Ripple - 2012) Stoner Rock

There are just some artists in rock that trudge along the landscape and after years of recording and touring, never quite crack the service outside of an underground, loyal fanbase. One of those bands is Mos Generator, who have been around since 2000. This trio is a combination of the best elements of Black Sabbath, grunge, doom and stoner rock. In 2012, *Nomads* was a record that clearly showcases all those traits. Add some blues and classic rock structures into the brew, and you have an album that should have been heard by more than just the underground. Highlight tracks on this album are the melodic groove infection of "Lonely One Kenobi," "Cosmic Ark" and the 70s Kiss styled "Solar Angels." Why this album, or band for that matter has been kept in the shadows is anyone's guess. Time to restart this generator and crank loud and proud. A very overlooked, underappreciated, and underrated album.

Mother's Finest – Iron Age (Atlantic - 1981) Funk Rock

Atlanta's funk rockers Mother's Finest was a rock band from the 1970's that combined funk, hard rock and some southern boogie to their music. They were building a modest following even opening for bands like Aerosmith and AC/DC. In 1981, they would release *Iron Age*, which would be the heaviest album they had released to date. Before *Iron Age*, the band's sound was more infused into pure funk rock, and the group had a hit on R&B radio with "Baby Love" in 1977. Led by vocalist Joyce Kennedy, who had enough soul to fill a room, was a solid vocalist. I will go on record to say that she may be one of the most underappreciated vocalists of her time. Glenn Murdock was another vocalist for the band. Having both female and male lead vocalists that didn't overshadow each other was another big plus for the band. Standout tracks include the Murdock led "U Turn Me On" which has a ZZ Top feel, the Kennedy led heavy blues rocker "Movin On" and the southern rocker "Earthling." This album was sort of caught in the crossroads for the band. As they wanted to rock. But the record label was hoping for the group to go more in an R&B direction and capture that demographic. As it would happen, neither rock or R&B would play the album and Mother's Finest would drift away from the scene outside of some additional records that failed to gain any traction.

Motley Crue – S/T (Elektra - 1994) Hard Rock

It's hard to argue that Motley Crue was probably one of the biggest names in rock/hard rock in the 1980's. However, disagreements within the band would force Vince Neil out and new vocalist John Corabi in. With a new singer in tow, this also changed the direction of the band's sound. They muscled up and gone were all the 80s hard rock/glam metal trappings found on their other albums (which I will add were still heavier than most in the genre at the time). Corabi was the perfect voice for this style. Which is evident on tracks like "Misunderstood," "Hooligan's Holiday" and "Smoke The Sky." This Motley Crue was a down-tuned monster and was doing no different than other artists from the 80s were doing at the time. What the major issue with this record is that it was a commercial failure compared to everything that preceded it. It was evident that fans were not happy with the change in musical direction or vocalists. Which is a shame because this album flat out rocks full throttle. Meanwhile, John Corabi's time in the band was short-lived, and Vince Neil was back. In 1996, the group would release *Generation Swine* and outside of a few tracks, falls flat compared to Corabi's underappreciated gem.

Motorhead – S/T (Chiswick - 1977) Hard Rock

As we all know, Lemmy is a legend. He may be one of the most recognizable names and faces when it comes to hard rock and metal. It would also be tough to find bands that don't claim Motorhead as an influence. However, let's get to facts, most casual fans of rock and hard rock genre, if they know Motorhead at all, it's because of the song "Ace of Spades" or for more modern looks, those times they did theme songs for WWE's Triple H. In the world of underrated bands, Lemmy and company may get a nod. Let's start at the beginning with the first Motorhead album. This is Motorhead in their rawest form and in 1977, they have a sound that is dark and low (similar to Black Sabbath) but also has a punk and blues feel. The band was on to something when they put this record out, and songs like "Motorhead," "Vibrator" and their cover of The Yardbirds "Train Kept A Rollin" were just the beginning for this band. However, by 1983, "Fast" Eddie Clarke would leave Motorhead to form Fastway, and Lemmy would carry on with Motorhead and build a legacy that would last until his passing. If you only know Motorhead by name and a few songs, then you need to begin with this album to get the real understanding of their existence and why so many people praise this band.

The Move – Shazam (A&M - 1970) Classic Rock

Before having eventual ties with Electric Light Orchestra, The Move was a favorite band in the UK. *Shazam* is the second release from the group, and it's an excellent blend of pop, hard rock, and psychedelic sounds. Beginning with the opening track, the pop-oriented "Hello Susie" and followed by the Beatlesque "Beautiful Daughter." This track also showed elements of string instruments which preceded E.L.O. and Jeff Lynne's actual contribution to the band (Roy Wood and Bev Bevan were in The Move during this time). Their psychedelic side shows on later tracks with songs clocking in over 6 minutes. The one song that stands out is the heavier track "Don't Make My Baby Blue," which one could see why bands like Cheap Trick were influenced by the band among others. Not a household name in the US, but they have had a pretty underground following forever and giving *Shazam* a listen is to see how influential The Move was.

N-P

Naked Raygun – Jettison (Caroline - 1988) Punk Rock

In the 80s was an authentic underground punk scene that was branching out into other various genres like hardcore, melodic hardcore and post-punk. While we are not here to go over specific definitions, the style led to very successful bands that clearly were influenced, like Nirvana and Helmet. Naked Raygun was one of the premier original bands of the genre, which combined punk rock/hardcore with melodies as well as traces of soul or jazz. Naked Raygun, who has members that would become the influential Big Black, had been around since 1980 and when they released *Jettison* in 1988. It was a unique showcase of where the sound of so many bands was heading in the 1990's. Beginning with "Soldiers Requiem," the band shows a brand of punk rock that is melodic and perfect to sing along or join the mosh pit. Still raw in production, it's unfortunate that they didn't see much coverage outside of college radio. Other songs like "Coldbringer" and "Free Nation" continue along the same lines. However, like so many other 80s punk/hardcore bands, the ones that didn't get picked up in the alternative rock wave of the 90s stayed in their plainly underground roots. Naked Raygun would press on but never really captured the success they deserved.

Nashville Pussy – High As Hell (TVT - 2000) Southern Rock

If there is one rock genre type that really gets a raw deal is southern rock and any of its numerous sub-genres (cowpunk, psychobilly to name a few). Here is another example of a band that has a love of punk and southern rock in Atlanta's Nashville Pussy. Now Georgia already has some very talented rock/ southern rock bands that don't always get the love like Drivin N Cryin and Jackyl, but you can add this band to the list. If you like Southern Rock, Punk, and lyrics full of sex and drugs, this is your band. They have rocked with both Lemmy of Motorhead and Danko Jones, so other musicians want to rock alongside them. In 2000, they released *High As Hell*, a follow-up to their Grammy-nominated *Let Them Eat Pussy*. Maybe this is one of those bands with a name we can't say on the radio that keeps people away. The music is infectious, from the southern sleaze rock of "Struttin Cock," to the quickness of "Shoot First And Run Like Hell." These songs and others clock in less than three minutes, which clearly appeals to the moshers in the pit. There are some longer rockers like the full throttle cruiser "Let's Ride." Nashville Pussy is a band that brings the party and don't care about offending anyone, be it a band name or lyrical content (or title for that matter). *High As Hell* is a sure-fire way to kick out the jams with this band.

Neds Atomic Dustbin – God Fodder (Sony - 1991) Alternative Rock

Back when I was in high school, I remember a local band from my hometown that played with two bass players. Of course, I had never seen anything like it before and didn't even recall any group that had done such a thing. Then in 1991, I discovered Ned's Atomic Dustbin. Then and still the only group I know that have two bass players (one is known as lead bass). When *God Fodder* was released, this UK band was coming into the US at just the right time with Nirvana taking over music, and all groups different from the norm were being snatched up to deals. Their sound was a mashup of power pop meets punk, melodic and structured one minute, and then out of control and distorted the next. While "Kill Your Television" had a brief MTV moment during its time, it's songs like "Selfish" and "Throwing Things" that show the best traits of what their sound was all about. What's unfortunate for Ned's Atomic Dustbin is the timing.

Grunge was taking over, and despite being different, they were still a lower tier band in the grand scheme. While they would put out a few more records that would do well on the college charts, they failed to make a dent here in the U.S.

Neil Young – Mirror Ball (Reprise - 1995) Classic Rock

When grunge music took over the world in the 1990's, Neil Young became the godfather. It was a very intriguing pairing when Neil Young teamed up with Pearl Jam to release Mirror Ball in 1995. With Young's past career matched up alongside a Seattle band with three top charting albums under their belt, it's like the ultimate dream. Add super-producer Brendan O' Brien to the mix and *Mirror Ball* is a true all-star team ready to make musical history. At the end of the day, it's a classic Neil Young record. Sure, it has somewhat of a Pearl Jam feel, but it's Young at the forefront. His voice, his guitar, his words. Some of the tracks that stand out from this album include the classic rock stomper "Downtown," the rolling feedback driven opener "Song X" sounds like a drinking sing along, while "I'm The Ocean" is a seven-minute bottom ended cruiser. Neil Young was never an artist to not take chances, he pretty much did everything from folk rock, hard rock, even new wave, and rockabilly. Teaming up with the top rock band of the time didn't seem like a stretch and was another notch in the Neil Young legacy. The album debuted #5 in the US but only managed to go gold. You would have thought the pairing alone would have made Mirror Ball an instant success and a highlight of Young's career. Even with a legacy as significant as Young's, you are likely to have plenty of over-looked gems in your time.

New England – S/T (Geffen - 1979) Rock

In the 1970's, the cool thing was to have a band name of a city or state. Some of the greats include Boston, Chicago, and Kansas to name a few. One of the bands you may have never heard of was New England, who released their debut album in 1979. New England was a melodic rock band that blended unique musical structures. They had elements of prog and Queen type influences in the music, which really stand out. New England's only Top 40 hit comes on "Don't Ever Want to Lose Ya," which is amazing that this song was not a Top 10 hit for the time. New England didn't stand out for some reason in 1979. Perhaps it has something to do with the amount of great music coming out at the time? Other tracks like "Hello, Hello, Hello" and "Nothing To Fear" could have been radio staples and the band should have been rubbing shoulders with artists like Styx. Instead, they became a band that drifted out of sight, and people missed a great sounding record.

Nickelback – The State (Roadrunner - 1999) Hard Rock

Before they became one of the biggest rock bands in the world and one of the biggest punching bags for haters, they were a rock band from Canada. With their second album, *The State*, they were falling into the "post-grunge" genre. This album is well before the slick hook driven songs that would make them superstars, but you could see the beginnings of where they were going. Excellent songwriting, a great sound that could constitute the best elements of grunge, metal, nu metal and classic rock, sometimes in the same song. The major songs that stand out are "Old Enough," "Diggin This" and the lead single "Leader Of Men." The framework for how future Nickelback songs was full steam ahead. It wouldn't be until 2001, when their #1 chart hit "How You Remind Me" would change the band's fortunes forever, but if you listened to *The State* before Nickelback became what they are, then you already knew they were going to be great for a long time.

The Nils – S/T (Profile - 1987) Punk Rock

Most people are probably not familiar with The Nils. For starters, they are a Canadian punk band that started back in the late 70s, performed with The Ramones and X. Meanwhile, artists like The Goo Goo Dolls, Meat Puppets, and Husker Du were influenced by them. However, they would not release their US debut until 1987. Their sound is a healthy mix of melodic power punk. They could play fast and aggressive and still stay in a melodic and controlled nature. Songs like "River Of Sadness," "When Love Puts On A Sad Face" and "Wicked Politician" all displayed a quality that radio playlists should have been filled with. However, the story goes that their label was known more for rap and hip hop and not rock, which could have put a damper on the band's success in the US. They had a little run amongst the college ranks, but even that didn't put a dent in the music spectrum. The Nils was one band that surely got missed in the 80s.

The Nils (photo by Jonathan Wenk)

Nothing More – The Few Not Fleeting (Vestia - 2009) Hard Rock

While Nothing More has become a successful rock band in the last five years, it's been a prolonged process for the Texas band. *The Few Not Fleeting* is the third release from the band featuring the unique vocal stylings of Johnny Hawkins, who previously served as the band's drummer (insert Phil Collins, and Dave Grohl comments here). While this is an album that is pretty much hard to find, it clearly serves as the perfect album showing the direction the band was taking their sound; a blending of hard and progressive rock with a healthy dose of metal and hardcore without overdoing it. Standout tracks include "Fat Kid," which is musically all over the place and even includes string instruments and various effects, the heavy melodic "Gone" and the progressive rock grooves of "Bullets And Blue Eyes." The musicianship from the band is on a different level, and Hawkins vocals have a very distinctive sound. It would take five more years for the group to make their commercial breakthrough with 2014's self-titled release, but Nothing More has aged like a fine wine, and *The Few Not Fleeting* is a great album to have a taste test with.

Operator – Soulcrusher (Atlantic – 2007) Hard Rock

Operator is a band comprised of actor/vocalist Johnny Strong and former Puddle of Mudd guitarist Paul Phillips. I still remember the first time hearing this band and thought it was new music from Soundgarden that nobody said was going to be released. Strong's vocals have a very close resemblance to Chris Cornell's that it's easy to mistake. Starting with the title track, it sounds like something that would have come from Soundgarden's Badmotorfinger. Other tracks like "Nothing To Lose" and "Delicate" follow the same bloodline of comparisons. However, just when you think this is a simple copycat band, think again. Operator has a great sound, and they do have some diverse range in their musical spectrum outside of what a band like Soundgarden brings to the table. Johnny Strong's voice is fantastic and displays excellent range. It's hard to believe that *Soulcrusher* failed to get more attention than it did. Operator has not done anything since and it would have been interesting to see what they could have done with a follow-up.

Orgy – Vapor Transmission (Reprise - 2000) Industrial Rock

Orgy was a nu metal/industrial rock band that coined their brand of music death pop. In 1998, they scored a significant hit with the cover of New Order's "Blue Monday." When *Vapor Transmission* was released in 2000, there were some expectations to exceed their previous release Candyass. *Vapor Transmission* contained a wide arrangement of electronic instruments and effects as well as distorted guitars and melody. Lead single "Fiction (Dreams In Digital)" was a highlight of the album that did well on radio and encompasses everything that was already mentioned about the band's sound. Other tracks like "Eva" displayed a Cure-esque quality, while "Re-Creation" had a distorted new wave feel about it. The album was the highest charting release in the band's collection. However, after this, Orgy was relegated to independent releases that never really came close to *Vapor Transmission*. Not sure why this album never did more, other than in a nu-metal scene that was beginning to run its course and Orgy was a natural casualty.

Our Lady Peace – Spiritual Machines (Columbia-2000) Alternative Rock

Our Lady Peace was always a band that seemed out of place and hard to classify. For one, they have been labeled as hard rock, alternative rock, and grunge band. In 1997 with their second album *Clumsy*, they became an alternative rock staple with songs like the title track, "4am" and "Superman's Dead." When it came to *Spiritual Machines*, it seemed like these modern rockers from Canada were channeling their inner Radiohead during recording. The album began to take the shape of a conceptual release and influenced by *The Age Of Spiritual Machines*, written by Raymond Kurzweil. In fact, Kurzweil records several short-spoken word tracks from his book. From a musical standpoint, it's a classic which nobody either heard and those who have, ignored. Just about every track on the disc is a must listen. While songs like the moody "In Repair," the alterna-radio friendly "Life" and the manic driven "Everyone's A Junkie" are just a piece of the puzzle, the acoustic-driven "Are You Sad" showers you with emotion. Vocalist Raine Maida writes some of his best lyrics and his vocals have always been an OLP staple, while Mike Turner (Guitars), Jeremy Taggart (drums) and Duncan Coutts (bass) may have displayed the best work of their careers on this release. The album failed to become the next OK Computer. In 2002, OLP released the post-grunge styled *Gravity* and had their first Top 10 single with 'Somewhere Out There".

Pallbearer – Foundations Of Burden (Profound Lore - 2014) Metal

Most people not familiar with doom metal may steer clear away from the genre, but many don't realize that they have been listening to bands like Pallbearer for years, going all the way back to Black Sabbath to more modern bands like Type O Negative and Down for example. Pallbearer is not a household name in the rock world. Which is a shame because they may be one of the best-kept secrets outside of their core audience. Their music is bottom heavy and slow. At the same time, very structured and melodic vocals take the music to a different level. On *Foundations Of Burden*, there are six songs and only one of those is under four minutes. Radio may have an issue playing songs like the ten-plus minute "Worlds Apart" or "Foundations." These are songs that played at loud volumes will make the house shake and have your neighbors calling the police. The one short track "Ashes" is a lighter track (lighter by the band's standards) and shows that the group is not always sold on stomping on your heart every moment. This is a band and album that needs to be played loud on speakers or through your headphones to get the accurate thunder of what Pallbearer bring to the table.

Papa Roach – lovehatetragedy (Dreamworks - 2002) Nu Metal

When Papa Roach released *Infest* in 2000, they instantly became one of the most popular bands in the nu-metal genre, led by the song "Last Resort." When the band would follow up with *lovehatetragedy* in 2002, there were plenty of fans puzzled by the results. First, what happened to the rap-metal that the band previously dished out? In fact, many fans were sort of taken back by the softer approach. Not to take away from anything, *lovehatetragedy* is an incredible album that is full of heavy, aggressive songs and vocalist Jacoby Shaddix ditches the rap to show off some skills which would become more of the band's sound for the rest of their career. There is plenty of headbanging songs like the opener "M-80 (Explosive Energy Movement)," and songs like "She Loves Me Not" still have plenty of nu groove metal power. It's songs like "Time and Time Again" that may throw fans off. A song that is obviously more radio friendly. While this album only went gold (*Infest* went 3X Platinum), future releases have been successful, and Papa Roach has drawn quite a niche in rock radio since. *lovehatetragedy* is the one album that does not seem to get much exposure these days, perhaps due to the change in direction after a mega record. Despite the results, Papa Roach is still a favorite band today. So maybe a change in direction or style was not a bad idea after all.

Pete Shelley – XL1 (Genetic - 1983) New Wave

Many people may know Pete Shelley as the vocalist for UK punk band The Buzzcocks. While that band had a more abrasive sound, Shelley's solo work focused more on electronic/new wave sounds and traded away his guitar for synthesizers. *XL1* was the second electronic release, and while many of the bands of the time were gaining more radio exposure, Shelley's sound was a little more experimental than the norm, which may have kept more people from giving it a listen. The first song "Telephone Operator" was a minor hit on the radio at the time and if you are a fan of synthesizer and drum machines, this is right in your wheelhouse. Other tracks like "You Know Better Than I Know" feature some guitar work mixed in with the synths while "Many A Time" has some very cool bass grooves. While Shelley's new wave/electronica sound was not as popular as others at the time, you can see where artists have taken similar ideas from his work. For a true fan of new wave music, it would be a must to check out *XL1* as well as his previous work, *Homosapien*.

Poundhound – Massive Grooves From The Electric Church Of Psychedelic Grungelism Rock Music (Metal Blade - 1998) Hard Rock

King's X has always been a band that can't catch a break. Not only does this trio put out great albums, but even their solo records (Dug Pinnick, Ty Tabor, and Jerry Gaskill have all put out releases) don't get much love. In Dug Pinnick's debut solo record, it shows where King's X gets their bite. Pinnick handles bass, guitars, and vocals on this album and it is full of power, funk, and melodies that only Dug can deliver. This is one record where the low end needs to be at its max just for the ear-rattling you will hear from Pinnick's down-tuned bass. Examples of this can be found on "Shake," "Soul" and "Psycho Love." It's a record where Pinnick could drop his guard both musically and lyrically. Also, his guitar work, while nobody is going to compare him to anyone, stands on its own and fits throughout this record. While there are other Poundhound and Dug solo releases out there, *Massive Grooves* stands out as the go-to record of any of his work outside King's X.

Pray For The Soul Of Betty – S/T (Koch - 2005) Hard Rock

Back when *American Idol* was one of the biggest shows on television, some fantastic singers came through and deemed the rockers. Of course, the biggest one was Chris Daughtry, who carved out a pretty good career. So how does Pray for The Soul of Betty tie-in? The band was fronted by *American Idol* finalist Constantine Maroulis. The album was released before Maroulis left to pursue an opportunity to win *American Idol*. As he became more popular, the band was eventually picked up by Koch Records, and they released this self-titled CD which managed to climb into the top 130 of Billboard. Overall, the recordings are not state of the art but for what you get is a fantastic record. The band's sound is somewhere between Stone Temple Pilots and Fuel. Maroulis shows a lot more grit vocally than when he was on the show. Check out the aggressiveness of "Drift," the acoustic stylings of "Truck Stop Sally" and the driving force of "Some of My F***d Up World." There was some definite potential, and it would have been great to see a follow-up. However, the band would tour, and in 2006, Maroulis would leave to record a solo record, which fell on deaf ears.

The Presidents of the United States of America – II (Columbia - 1996) Alternative Rock

Here is one band that after one album, had some big shoes to fill. Coming out of the Seattle scene, years after all the prominent grunge bands, The Presidents of the USA obviously were part of groups that got picked up once artists like Weezer became successful. Let's face facts, bands that had odd lyrics, punk/hard rock/pop styles were the rage. In 1995, they exploded onto the scene with songs like "Lump" and "Peaches," and the alterna-kids couldn't get enough of it. In 1996, not to waste any time, released *II*. The results are about the same: A three-piece band that combined punk rock with alternative rock, weird lyrics and mostly done in less than 3 minutes. While songs like "Mach 5", "Tiki God" and "Volcano" displayed the formula of their previous release, the band never came close to the success. The Presidents would continue to rock but are still known for their debut hits. Could the Presidents of the USA be the 90s version of Devo? That could be an interesting question.

Puya – Fundamental (MCA - 1999) Nu Metal

While there are plenty of bands that have put out various genres of music and combined them as one, I don't believe anyone ever thought, "I'd like some salsa with my metal." In 1999, that changed and Puya was a band with enough balls to pull it off. Hailing from Puerto Rico, they would release *Fundamental* and would turn hard rock and metal on their head. There was nothing on this record they wouldn't put together. It's a concoction of metal, salsa, alternative rock, rap, and even jazz. Better take a few Spanish lessons because the boys in Puya sing in both English and Espanol, which brings another intrigue to their music. Bring a partner, because in songs like the title track, one minute you will be dancing before slamming around in the mosh pit the next. Other tracks that embrace this feeling include "Whatever" and "Oasis." So, the question is why didn't Puya become huge? Maybe they were too much for anyone to fully embrace. Perhaps they were just way out there musically. Whatever it was, they were one of the more creative artists coming out of a time where Limp Bizkit and Kid Rock were beginning to rule the rock scene, and *Fundamental* fell on lost ears.

Jim Santora Jr

Q-R

Queensryche – American Soldier (Rhino - 2009) Progressive Metal

American Soldier was a concept album that revolved around the story of war and the experiences of those people who proudly served in the US Military. Probably the best part of the record are the parts where actual soldiers that ranged from World War II to the Iraq War shared stories, either at the beginning or ends of songs or as part of actual tracks. While the album did manage to crack the Top 25 album charts, it pales in comparison to albums like *Empire* or *Operation: Mindcrime*. This album has some very proud moments and some of the band's most heartfelt songs. Songs like the hypnotic "Hundred Mile Stare," the very realistic thoughts of war in "Middle Of Hell" and the heartbreak of being away in "Home Again," which features Geoff Tate's daughter on vocals. This is an album that is full of emotions and is a tribute to those who sacrifice for the rest of us. Tate's vision was off the charts with this album. This is an album that anyone who appreciates what the military does for our freedoms needs to give a listen.

R.E.M. – Monster (Warner Bros - 1994) Alternative Rock

By the time *Monster* is released, R.E.M. already had locked themselves in as one of the best modern/alternative rock bands of all time. They were one of the more popular bands of their genre and broke big in 1987 with the hit single "The One I Love." From there, they had quite a run with 1989's *Green*, 1991's *Out of Time* and 1992's *Automatic For The People*. In 1994, R.E.M. release *Monster*, which despite going 4X platinum to date, this album does not get the same treatment as the albums that precede it. For one, the band got a little louder with Monster. Gone was some of the soft, jangle pop they were famous for. The band seemed proud to embrace this new sound in songs like "Bang And Blame" and "Crush With Eyeliner." Not to worry, as the band did bring out the ballads with "Strange Currencies," which also is louder in tone. *Monster* is one of those albums that gets lost in a pile of other great R.E.M. records. If you want to remember when R.E.M. wanted to rock, then you need to pull this out of the collection.

Raging Slab – S/T (RCA - 1989) Southern Rock

Raging Slab before their major label debut was a New York band with a love of 70s bands like Mountain, "boogie rock" and punk rock like the Ramones and Black Flag. Their independent releases like *Assmaster* and *True Death* showed both sides. Didn't hurt that you also were part of a scene that included White Zombie and Monster Magnet. Raging Slab was the first of those bands signed to a major label and in 1989 came their self-titled release. Raging Slab doesn't get a lot of love in the world of southern rock, but this album stands up to the best albums of the genre (Maybe it's a New York thing?). If you are a fan of southern (or for that matter stoner) rock, you need to listen to a record that has plenty of catchy grooves and enough drive to blow the horn on your semi. Stand out tracks include the first single "Don't Dog Me," "Waitin For The Potion" the powerful "Shiny Mama" (featuring Ray Gillan on background vocals) and the slower chugger in "Geronimo." This is an ultimate get out on the highway and cruise record. The highlight is the slide guitar work of Elise Steinman, which never disappoints on any song from this record. A hardcore audience would love to see more from the band. Sadly, Steinman passed away in 2017 after a battle with cancer.

Ratt – S/T (Sony - 1999) Hard Rock

Ratt was one of the biggest names in the hard rock 80s. Thanks to hits like "Round and Round," the band was one of the first bands out of the L.A. scene to break it big, along with Motley Crue, Quiet Riot, and Dokken. Ratt was on a hiatus/breakup for a good part of the 90s, so when they got an opportunity to jump back on a major label, they came out with this self-titled release in 1999, their eighth if you count the debut EP. Many people think Ratt was nothing more than a one trick pony over the course of their career, but with this release, they break the mold showing a more mature rock sound than the let's party and hang out with hot chick's atmosphere of prior releases. Standout tracks include "Over The Edge," "Live For Today" and "Tug Of War." While this album was not well received when released and became the first of their major label albums to not go gold status, it is an album that shows the band continued to grow with age.

Recovery Council – Gentle Stories (DotUltra - 2011) Alternative Rock

Recovery Councils *Gentle Stories* was a breath of fresh air in 2011. As the album itself takes us back to a time where bands like Dinosaur Jr, Pixies, and Squirrel Bait were still cutting their teeth before the great 90s alternative music explosion. Recovery Council's sound would have fit perfectly in with those and so many other bands from that time. More importantly, Recovery Council was a one-person show in Rebecca Qualls. Qualls sings, play guitars, bass, and keyboards as well as some electronic drums and various programming. She also handled all or most of the engineering/mixing of the album which is an even more significant achievement for such an incredible sounding record. Stand out tracks include the grungy pop of "Wool," "Runner-Up" and "A Million Questions" a cover from the band My Dad Is Dead, which is a combination of soft keyboards and punk rock which is an excellent closer for this disc. Recovery Council is probably more of an unknown band to most but who knows what could have happened if more ears were given the opportunity to hear this album. *Gentle Stories* is a winner in the DIY musician and production category.

Rebeca Qualls of Recovery Council (photo courtesy of the artist)

Red Hot Chili Peppers – The Uplift Mofo Party Plan (Capitol - 1987) Funk Rock

While they are considered the most decorated alternative rock band, most fans and people only know their body of work from the 90s forward. The Red Hot Chili Peppers began as a funk rock band in the 80s and in 1987 released *The Uplift Mofo Party Plan.* The music is infectious as they mix punk and metal into their funk rock style. Most of the songs feature Flea showing why he is considered one of the best bassists of his time as well as late guitarist Hillel Slovak, who is a very underrated guitarist in his own right. Then there is vocalist Anthony Kiedis, whose voice shows excellent range flowing between funk and rock styles, even touching hip-hop at times. Standout tracks include "Fight Like A Brave," "Backwoods" and "Organic Anti-Beat Box Band." While this release would be a standout on college radio, RHCP would begin to reap some success with 1989's *Mother's Milk* and eventually become one of the biggest bands on the planet with *Blood, Sugar, Sex, Magic* in 1991.

Redlight King – Irons In The Fire (Hollywood - 2013) Modern Rock

In 2011, Redlight King came onto the music scene with *Something For The Pain* and had some success thanks to songs like "Bullet In My Hand" and the Neil Young-inspired "Old Man." The buzz was going strong with this artist, and in 2013 Redlight King released *Irons In The Fire*. This album was more of a rocker compared to their debut. It is obvious that the band wanted to rock and with songs like the anthem "Born To Rise," the Stone Temple Pilots styled "Devil's Dance" and the southern sounds of "Wipe The Floor With You." The album has a great vibe, but it did not take the band to the next level. The result would be that the group left Hollywood Records and put out an EP in 2015 that did not catch anyone's attention outside of their hardcore fans.

Red Line Chemistry – Tug Of War (Bulldog - 2013) Hard Rock

Hard Rock in the 2010's is tough to break. Especially when we are seeing everything going pop/hip-hop everything. Solid melodic hard rock bands are tough to come by. For every Pop Evil and Red Sun Rising, there is a band like Red Line Chemistry, that has all the talent to be a top tier force in rock but continue to take a backseat. Let's bring you to exhibit A in their 2013 release *Tug of War*. This is an album that says play me often as soon as you crank it up. Not only are we talking about excellent musicianship and vocalist Brett Ditgen as one of the most underrated and unknown singers out there but Grammy-winning producer Nick Raskulinecz (Foo Fighters, Rush, Alice In Chains) was operating controls. Songs like "Paralyzed," "Sucker Punch" and "Unspoken" should have been radio staples but instead were cast off as mid-card tracks. Another band, another album that needs to be re-introduced to the masses.

Red Rider – Neruda (Capitol - 1983) Rock

For most people, mention Red Rider and if they are familiar with the band will quickly say "Lunatic Fringe." Also need to know that Tom Cochrane (that's right, the "Life Is A Highway" song) was lead vocalist for the band. While "Lunatic Fringe" is still a popular song today (released in 1981), Red Rider rode a wave of success coming into 1983's release *Neruda*. Red Rider's sound crosses the boundaries of classic and prog rock with a pinch of what the 80s brought us with heavy synth structures. While songs like "Human Race" gained some airplay upon its release, and "Can't Turn Back" was used in an episode of *Miami Vice*, it didn't generate enough to take Red Rider to that next level of success, despite crafting some great lighter melodic rock songs. Another standout track includes "Winner Take All," which is a little more rock influenced, complete with Cochrane's controlled melodic vocals and in step synths and rhythm section. Red Rider stuck around for most of the 80s and had some moderate success. However, they were one of those "one hit wonders" at the end of the day, and people should listen to *Neruda* one more time to see what they missed.

Reo Speedwagon – Good Trouble (Epic - 1982) Classic Rock

The history of Reo Speedwagon goes back to 1967. A band that grinded through the 70s and had some success with songs like "Time For Me to Fly" and "Roll With The Changes." Then in 1980 they finally scored with *Hi Infidelity*. All the band's hard work paid off with hit singles and radio staples "Keep on Loving You" and "Take It On the Run." This group of Midwesterners became one of the biggest bands of the early 80s. When it came time for a follow-up, they would release *Good Trouble* in 1982. This album is a classic example of an overlooked album over time. Sure, the album is the band's second-biggest seller behind *Hi Infidelity* and is led by the hit single and opening track "Keep The Fire Burning." Meanwhile, other tracks like "The Key" and "I'll Follow You" all have that Reo Speedwagon feel, more polished than ever of course. That does not take away that this was not a great band with yet another solid release. However, like so many other artists that made that huge crossover from rock to pop radio, the quest for every song to be a hit is always going to be what drives a record label moving forward. I believe this is the major issue with *Good Trouble* and its longevity. I do not hear anything from this album on classic rock radio. Meanwhile, 80s-oriented stations pretty much are hooked on the previously mentioned *Hi Infidelity* tracks and of course the pop classic "Can't Fight This Feeling."

Kevin Cronin and Neil Doughty of Reo Speedwagon (photo by Byron Crowley)

Ric Ocasek – Beatitude (Geffen - 1982) Classic Rock

The Cars are one of the premier new wave/rock bands of all time. In the early 80s, guitarist/vocalist Ric Ocasek stepped away from the group to release his first solo effort *Beatitude.* The album itself is more of a creative twist away from what he was doing with the band, but one can see what makes Ocasek an excellent songwriter. The biggest song from the album is "Something To Grab For," which could have easily fit on any Cars album and served as a Top 5 Rock Hit, which rarely gets heard from today. The rest of the album had more keyboards and an experimental feel, as songs like "Jimmy Jimmy" and "Out of Control" fit that mix perfectly. The album would break the Top 30, but unless you were a massive fan of The Cars, you probably do not own or have even listened to this album. This is just a dotted line to what Ric has done as a songwriter, and it's a definite re-listen, or for that matter, new listen.

Robert Bradley's Blackwater Surprise – S/T (RCA - 1996) Blues Rock

While the 90s was a hotbed for grunge and alternative rock, there was a resurgence of blues style rock as well. With bands like the Black Crowes, Blues Traveler, and Hootie & The Blowfish paving the way. Even Tracy Chapman was making a comeback during the time. So, in the mix was a Detroit band known as Robert Bradley's Blackwater Surprise. It's really a great story of Robert Bradley, a blind musician who by the time this debut came out in 1996, was 46 years old. The better late than never motto couldn't fit better for this group. Their music was in the form of R&B, rock, and soul, with some funk for good measure. For people that might remember them, you would be familiar with "Once Upon A Time," which did get some video play on MTV and VH1. Other tracks like "Bellybone" and "Burn" are just a sampling of songs that take you back in the time of the R&B greats of the late 60s and 70s. Which may be a reason that more people did not pay attention to the group. While the music is excellent, the sound may have been a little dated for 1996. Which is a shame because Robert Bradley has a voice that could reach into you, draw you in and make you listen to every note. A surprise indeed for anyone that picks up this album to give a listen.

The Runaways – Waitin On The Night (Mercury - 1977) Alternative Rock

Over the years, The Runaways had gotten more press and accolades post-breakup than when they were together in the late 70s. Of course, the band features Hall of Famer Joan Jett and "Kiss Me Deadly" Lita Ford. They were also known for the song "Cherry Bomb," which was not a huge hit in the US back in 1976, has made its way to popularity thanks to some movie soundtracks over the years. By the time *Waitin On The Night* was released in 1977, Jett had taken over as lead vocalist. It is surprising how this band never really took off. The Runaways are a straight-up hard rock band that brings it on songs like "Wasted" and "School Days," then go Black Sabbath on "Fantasies." Maybe it was the thought of an all-female band rocking out that scared people? Or was it that people didn't know if they were a hard rock or punk rock band? Regardless, the group became the springboard for Jett and Ford, and they also influenced artists like the Go-Go's, Vixen and L7 to follow as all female artists into the rock world.

Run DMC – Crown Royal (Arista - 2001) Rap Rock

Now I am sure there will be people scratching their head at this selection but let's lay down some facts. Run DMC was one of the first hip-hop artists that used rock tracks and beats into their music. They also teamed up with Aerosmith and revived their career. Finally, by the time *Crown Royal* was released in 2001, there is an onslaught of nu-metal/rap metal bands taking over the rock landscape. This album was just a matter of time. We have Rev. Run, DMC, Jam Master J and a host of guests. The results are a rock and rap montage that is a fun listen. Of course, this album did not get much play on rock radio. But that's not the point. This is an album showcasing one of the premier hip-hop artists, legends of the genre rocking out with the likes of Fred Durst, Everlast, Kid Rock and Stephan Jenkins of Third Eye Blind. Stand out tracks include "Rock Show," "Take the Money and Run" and "Here We Go 2001" featuring Sugar Ray. This may be a highly underappreciated album in the group's collection. Run DMC has influenced as many rock artists as they have hip-hop, which is why this album needs to be unearthed and given another listen.

Rush – Grace Under Pressure (Mercury - 1984) Progressive Rock

The biggest problem with a band like Rush is which album of the band's Hall of Fame career is underrated, underappreciated and overlooked. If the book didn't have an only one record per band criteria, you could bet there would have been multiple Rush albums taking their place. In the end, *Grace Under Pressure* is the hidden gem out of a list of fantastic albums. Released in 1984, it comes after a trio of incredible releases (*Permanent Waves*, *Moving Pictures*, and *Signals*). At the beginning of the 80s, the trio went away from conceptual releases and began a wave of radio rotation classics. This was also the time when new wave music was big, and Rush was embracing more keyboard synths as well as adding ska music into their progressive rock sound. Beginning with the opening track "Distant Early Warning," with swirling soundscapes, layered synths and excellent musicianship open an incredible album. Other tracks like "Kid Gloves" show off more guitars as Geddy Lee's synths take more of a backing roll to show off more of Alex Lifeson's talents. Another solid song is the closing track "Between The Wheels," where everything comes together, and the band shows off their ultimate skills. Through it all, Neil Peart shows why he is one of the greatest drummers to ever step behind a kit. While there are some fantastic songs on this album, they do not get the airplay on classic rock radio as others from the records before this. Some fans were not in favor of the direction the band was heading at the time, *Grace Under Pressure* begins that trend. Going away from the prog metal they pretty much invented. Rush was a band that was never afraid of changing up, and they were always influenced by much more and still learning. The 80s would not be very kind to the band, but thanks to loyal fans, they would carve a pretty good path for themselves and still be one of the most talented groups on the planet for another 30 years after this release.

Alex Lifeson and Geddy Lee of Rush (photo by Byron Crowley)

S-T

Saliva – Survival Of The Sickest (Island - 2004) Hard Rock

At the time of this release, Saliva was riding a successful run amongst the giants of nu metal. With songs like "Your Disease," "Click Click Boom" and "Always" from their first two major releases, *Survival Of The Sickest* was sure to be more of the same. Josey Scott and company come out even heavier than before and drop the rap stylings that was a major part of their previous releases. Saliva brought out more of an edge on these tracks, beginning with the title track which is balls to the wall heart pounding hard rock. Another track that stands out is "Two Steps Back," which lyrically steps into some life and event issues like 9/11. Even the Dixie Chicks got called out for actions they did back at that time. The band even finds some southern rock roots in "Razor's Edge" which makes sense for a hard rock/metal band hailing from the Carolina's. This was a band and an album where the group stepped out of their norm of prior releases. While many of the tracks may not be Saliva's staples amongst their best or most popular songs, *Survival Of The Sickest* stands out as their most potent and surefire underdog in the catalog.

Sebastian Bach – Kicking and Screaming (Frontiers - 2011) Hard Rock

Let's end all arguments right now. Sebastian Bach is Skid Row! His vocal stylings before his departure from the band in 1996 are what made that band what they were. Bach would not release a solo record until 2007's *Angel Down* and then wait another four years to release *Kicking And Screaming*. On this record, Bach shows what made him one of the most recognized vocalists in hard rock. While the songs are not always as in your face or heavy as Skid Row, Bach and his band throw down some great hard rock. Some of the stand out tracks include "Tunnelvision," which really shows off his range, the cruising "As Long As I've Got The Music" and the heaviness of "Dance On Your Grave," which might be the closest to sounding like a lost track from Skid Row. There is never denying the vocal talents of Sebastian Bach and *Kicking And Screaming* sure stands out. Of course, like most other hard rock 80s bands, they fell out of favor a long time ago, so you probably didn't hear any of these songs on the radio or even realize that Bach was even releasing albums. He is still kicking ass.

Jim Santora with Sebastian Bach (photo by Jennifer Hickman)

Seven Circle Sunrise – Beauty In Being Alone (Self Released - 2011) Hard Rock

One of the more unknown bands to make this list is Cleveland's Seven Circle Sunrise. Their sound is comparable to another underrated band, Smile Empty Soul but that's where the similarities end. Led by Veno Xavier, the songs on *Beauty In Being Alone* are on a very personal level. Musically, the band is full on hard rock, yet very melodic and I'm sure the post-grunge labels exist. Lyrically, it's very thought-provoking, and anyone that has dealt with loss and various tragedies in their lives can relate. Tracks that show a true impact on this album include "After All," "Broken Man" and "Another Day." Overall, a compelling record, yet it never caught on to the mainstream. One of the best self-released albums that people probably have never heard of. Which begs to question why none of the labels ever latched on? So many questions, but the band still performs, and the album is available for ears to continue to listen.

Shaman's Harvest – Smokin Hearts and Broken Guns (Mascot - 2014) Southern Rock

Upon writing this, *Smokin Hearts And Broken Guns* seems to have gotten some late popularity thanks to eventual radio airplay a year after its release. Lumped in with the post-grunge bands, they are simply a hard rock band with a definite southern rock influence. This album is a great listen from top to bottom. From the southern vibes of "Blood In The Water," the country-rock fueled feel, and high energy of "Country As F***," and even their cover of Michael Jackson's "Dirty Diana" comes off as a tremendous mid-tempo southern blues number. Shaman's Harvest is a very talented band and needs to be delivered to a much broader audience. In 2017, they released *Red Hands Black Deeds* and secured a supporting spot with Nickleback. So, the band is getting exposure, giving them a fighting chance. Hopefully, they continue to generate some steam moving forward.

Shooting Star – Hang On For Your Life (Virgin - 1981) Classic Rock

Shooting Star was a Midwestern rock band that for the most part, was a middle-tiered band in the early 1980's. Their albums cracked into the Billboard charts, and the band toured with everyone from Journey to John Mellencamp. With their second release, *Hang On For Your Life* had a true midwestern feel like many of the groups that came before them, which was a cross of ZZTop, Reo Speedwagon, and Kansas. The title track may be the most recognizable track from the band and was a minor radio hit. Other tracks like "Flesh and Blood" had a Kansas-esque feel with the use of the violin in the song. While a song like "Breakout" is pure boogie rock. Perhaps the reason this album and the band, in general, didn't get a more significant break or become more recognizable is that of identity. This album had some great songs, but the direction had them at times playing two different styles, which may have confused people. Despite that, this is an excellent record that needs to be listened to again.

Shotgun Messiah – Violent New Breed (Relativity - 1993) Industrial Rock

While bands like Ministry were leading a new genre in music with industrial rock/metal, there were plenty of other groups in the 90s that would embrace the sounds and gravitate towards success. While artists like White Zombie, Nine Inch Nails, and Orgy in the late 90s enjoyed success, several bands were virtually ignored. One of those was Swedish band Shotgun Messiah. The group was a moderate successful hard rock (hair band) in the late 80s as that style was starting its decline. By 1993, the group had incorporated an industrial rock sound into their music, and the result was *Violent New Breed*. Not sure where the influences came from, but it was a definite turn from what they sounded like before. While songs like "I'm A Gun," "Enemy In Me" and "Jihad" show a band that evidently changed its approach, a deep listen show a group that still stays true to their 80s sound, squeezed down in the mix of course. While this album is a curious listen and a band taking risks, it would be evident how fans of the band's earlier work may have turned away. It would also appear *Violent New Breed* still has a little too much 80s bounce for the Industrial and 90s rockers to enjoy, so they passed. That does not mean it has to be avoided today.

Skid Row – Subhuman Race (Atlantic - 1995) Hard Rock

By the mid-90s, bands from the glam metal 80s were just about dead and buried. That did not mean that all the groups were going to go down without a fight. Skid Row was one of those bands. Four years removed from the very heavy *Slave To The Grind*, which was a #1 album for them, the band took their time in releasing *Subhuman Race*. The timing could have been the one thing that stopped this record from being another major player in the hard rock world. Some great songs combined the heavy metal elements that made them what they are. With this album, they stepped up their sound including touches of grunge, thrash and groove metal. Put that together with the amazing vocal abilities of Sebastian Bach, and this is a can't miss record. Standout tracks include the head banging "Beat Yourself Blind," the melodic "Into Another" and the grunge-inspired "Eileen." It was unfortunate that many fans had jumped off the Skid Row bandwagon in 1995 because they missed a great album. Even critics gave it positive reviews. It was after this release that Skid Row sadly imploded. Sebastian Bach was forced out of the band and Skid Row, despite several releases over the years, has never come close to their past, which includes this hidden diamond in the rough.

Slade – Slayed? (Polydor - 1972) Glam Rock

Not a household name in the US, but Slade was a favorite band in the UK with their brand of glam rock in the 70s. In fact, it wasn't until the 1980's that the group would actually be known thanks to Quiet Riot's covers of "Cum On Feel The Noise" and "Mamma Weer All Crazee Now", than for their 80s hits "Run Runaway" and "My Oh My". Slade is a very straight up sound, which has a combination of pop-oriented hard rock. With songs like "Gudbuy T'Jane," "How D'you Ride" and of course "Mamma Weer All Crazee Now," it's not hard to see why bands like Kiss, Twisted Sister, and even Nirvana cite Slade as an influence. Not always very polished and *Slayed?* is a raw hard rock/power popish record. Slade is not a band that makes many best of lists, but one that has a dotted line to so many great bands they influenced.

Smash Into Pieces – The Apocalypse DJ (Gain - 2015) Hard Rock

Popular in their home country of Sweden, Smash Into Pieces are a high energy melodic hard rock band that released *The Apocalypse DJ* in 2015. Looking at the album cover makes you first believe this band is more dubstep or EDM type electronica, but one needs to put this album on to witness what is truly a band that needs some attention. Every song has a very melodic, danceable structure. Some of the tracks to really pay attention to are the power ballad "Checkmate," the melodic cruiser "Disaster Highway" and the amazing duet "My Cocaine" featuring Elize Rud from the band Amaranthe. Overall, this is an album that sort of got cast away in the US, which was a shame. This is one bound to be classified in the unknown but should be known for sure. Smash Into Pieces are still releasing music but still known more in Europe than North America.

The Smashing Pumpkins – Gish (Caroline - 1991) Alternative Rock

The Smashing Pumpkins are probably one of the most successful bands from the 90s along with Pearl Jam, Nirvana, Stone Temple Pilots and Alice In Chains. Before the multi-million selling albums, there was *Gish*, which is a true independent gem that usually does not get the praise it deserves. While the industry would eventually lump the band in with the grunge scene, the foursome from Chicago was anything but, combining goth, psychedelic, metal, and prog. All under the careful guidance of Billy Corgan, *Gish* brings all these styles and molds them into moments of angst which then turns magical. From the heavy rock of "Siva," the prog style of

"Rhinoceros" and the psychedelic ballad "Crush." Corgan was one of the best songwriters of the time, proving why following albums *Siamese Dream* and *Mellon Collie And The Infinite Sadness* took the band to superstar status. *Gish* is the album that started it all and one that should not be ignored. For any new fan of The Smashing Pumpkins, they should start at the beginning.

Smile Empty Soul – Vultures (Bieler Bros - 2006) Hard Rock

Another band to surely be considered as one of the most underrated and underappreciated in rock history. Smile Empty Soul have been on 5 or 6 labels, pretty much a different record company per album. That makes you wonder what their problems were with the band. Back in 2004, the band released probably their most recognizable song "Bottom Of The Bottle" and things looked up for the band. Instead, this band grinds out great music for 10+ years to a cult-like following. It's hard to find the one album that needs to find new ears. That brings us to *Vultures*, which track for track is a powerful album. Smile Empty Soul is a three-piece band that brings the rock that gives an obvious influence of 90s grunge rock combined with the ever-changing scene of alternative and nu-metal sounds. The difference is in vocalist/guitarist Sean Danielsen, who is an amazing songwriter and the perfect vocalist for these tracks. Just listen to tracks like "The Hit," "Adjustments" and "Here's To Another" and you will understand the magic this band brings. Each song is gripping both in sound, tone and the lyrical content is honest and real. Next thing you know, you are hooked. You could pretty much start anywhere in Smile Empty Soul's collection, but Vultures is a great entry if you are new to the band.

The Smithereens – Green Thoughts (Capitol - 1988) Alternative Rock

While the mid-80s was where glam metal was king. There was an alternative rock movement beginning. From the emergence of R.E.M. breaking into mainstream rock to artists like Husker Du, Red Hot Chili Peppers and Soul Asylum working their way up as well. New Jersey's The Smithereens were also in the mix. With the release of *Green Thoughts* in 1988, they already were a staple on the college charts and the song "Blood And Roses" gave the band some promise. One thing that stands out with The Smithereens, in general, is the songwriting of Pat DiNizio. One of the most underrated songwriters of our time. The emotions that he could lay down in words, with a band that could be soft and balladry one moment, then rock as hard as any of the heavy bands of the time. Most of the songs on *Green Thoughts* are not happy by any stretch. There are plenty of broken hearts, and people listening could relate to on these 11 tracks. From the rocking opener "Only A Memory", the head bobbing "Drown In My Own Tears" and the jangly psychedelic sounds of "Spellbound", it's a musical landscape for anyone missing the boy/girl of their dreams and realizing it's over. Never really sure why this album did not get the popularity it deserved like say R.E.M.'s *Green*. The band would need to wait until 1989 for their ultimate break and the song that would get them to the pinnacle of their success, "A Girl Like You."

Soul Asylum – Hang Time (A&M - 1988) Alternative Rock

Another band that most people did not know until their smash hit "Runaway Train" in 1992. Before Soul Asylum was going multi-platinum, they were a rock band from Minnesota combining their mix of Midwestern rock with punk and at times countrified rock. By the time *Hang Time* was released, they were on their fourth album. The songs on *Hang Time* are not far removed from what people would become mega fans of in the 90s. As tracks like "Sometime To Return," "Cartoon" and "Down On Up To Me" were as radio-ready as material that was coming up in their future. The problem was that Soul Asylum was still a staple to college radio and continued to build their way up. However, *Hang Time* is a clearly overlooked album in the band's collection.

Sound Barrier – Total Control (MCA - 1982) Hard Rock

While the Sunset Strip was just beginning to make some noise in the rock/hard rock scene of the 80s with bands like Motley Crue, Quiet Riot, Ratt, and Dokken, there was another band also paving a trail in many ways. Sound Barrier is what some have called the first all-black rock band. This generated some interest and press early on. Here was a group that is six plus years ahead of Living Colour, cranking out melodic hard rock, with elements of funk thrown in for good measure. In 1982, the band would sign to MCA and release *Total Control*. The sky was the limit from here, especially when you hear songs like the infectious "Rock Without The Roll," which may be the band's most recognized song thanks years later to when Metal Mania was on the now-defunct VH1 Classic. Other tracks that rocked include the title track and "Second Thoughts." Many of the songs on Total Control had so much more in common with Judas Priest that it's evident the band was influenced by them. However, this album came and went with not much that a blip on the radar. Sound Barrier was dropped by MCA, and future releases didn't do much to help their cause. While the sound didn't break barriers, their influence eventually would.

Soundgarden – Louder Than Love (A&M - 1989) Hard Rock

While most fans of Soundgarden didn't find the band until 1994, the group got its start back in 1987. By 1989, the group moved over to A&M and released *Louder Than Love*, an album that slowly put Soundgarden in the right direction. The band combined the heaviness of what would become grunge with elements of punk, metal and even some experimental structures to their mix. The group still had not fine-tuned their sound until 1991's Badmotorfinger, but it's evident that the group had something nobody else was doing at the time. Excellent musicianship and singer Chris Cornell was the best vocalist of what would become 90s alternative rock or grunge. Standout tracks are "Get On The Snake," "Big Dumb Sex" and "Hands All Over." *Louder Than Love* would be a standout on the college charts and the visible stepping stone to their top tier status heading into the 90s. This was an album where Soundgarden got their teeth, and the bite was hard.

Squirrel Bait – S/T (Homestead - 1985) Punk Rock

While punk music gets its start in the 70s, by the 1980's, new punk bands are emerging and putting a new spin on the music in general. Still, a precursor to grunge music, bands like Nirvana really are no different than groups like Husker Du, Big Black, and Dinosaur Jr. before them. Make sure you add Squirrel Bait to that list as well. On this self-titled album from 1985, this group from Louisville played high energy punk music that also incorporated what would eventually be known as melodic hardcore and emocore. With songs like "Sun God," "Hammering So Hard" and "Mixed Blessing," it's a wonder what this band could have done if they hadn't broken up in 1988. They were fast, full of angst and raw, with a blend of melody and chaos. This album, like so many other bands from this time, was not always high-quality production and that's a good thing about what Squirrel Bait brought to the table. Again, it's too bad we didn't see what this band could do during the grunge explosion, my money is that they could have been right there with Nirvana.

Starz – Violation (Capitol - 1977) Hard Rock

The 1970's had plenty of great rock and hard rock bands that dominated the musical landscape. Which means that groups like Starz fall through the cracks and were pretty much cast aside. They had a melodic hard rock/power pop style that is obvious, showing the musical landscape evolving in the 1980's. In 1977 when *Violation* was released, they had a minor hit with "Cherry Baby," which opens the record. The band has great melodic qualities, but their style was a little different than other bands in their genre. If you pay close attention, they almost seem like an American version of April Wine, which is not a negative. This is evident in songs like "Sing It, Shout It" and "All Night Long." Their musical structures also hint at Kiss and Aerosmith, but Starz was their own thing. It's too bad Starz did not continue into the 80s, they were a band that had real potential. Interesting note, members of Starz were in the early 70s band Looking Glass. Yes, the one that did "Brandy (You're A Fine Girl). Use that in your next music trivia conversation with your friends.

Stars (photo courtesy of the band)

Styx – Cornerstone (A&M - 1979) Classic Rock

The first question when everyone sees this album in the book will be the following: "How can you have this album on this list when it has a song like Babe"? Well here is a question, how many other songs do you know from this album? *Cornerstone* is the album between *Pieces Of Eight* and the classic *Paradise Theatre*. Sure, this album made it to #2 on the charts thanks to the ballad "Babe," but no other song reached the Top 40. Cornerstone is loaded with plenty of classic songs like the melodic, progressive and powerful "Why Me" and the acoustic-driven "Boat On The River." By this time in the band's career, they were firing on all cylinders. Incredible vocals from Dennis DeYoung and Tommy Shaw, and musically, one of the tightest groups on the planet. One glaring issue in 1979, this was one album where a song was so big that it overtook the whole record, which is never a bad thing, just meant that there were plenty of songs that got clearly overlooked. Fear not, Styx comes back blazing with multiple hits on 1981's *Paradise Theatre*.

Sugar – Copper Blue (Rykodisc - 1992) Alternative Rock

There is always an element of discussion as to when the real modern rock movement shifted. Of course, there are the people who say Nirvana's *Nevermind* was what started everything. Or was that when it exploded? Could it have been Jane's Addiction in 1989? Or was it Bob Mould's Husker Du? Husker Du was an explosive punk/melodic hardcore band in the 80s that caught their break in 1987 with a major label release. However, that lasted long enough for a cup of coffee as that band imploded and Mould recorded some solo releases that made the rounds of college radio. When the 90s begin, Mould formed Sugar and in 1992, released *Copper Blue*. Mould has a niche for amazing edgy power pop, and that shines throughout this release. Standout tracks like the bouncy "A Good Idea," the heavy power pop of "Changes" and the jangle stylings of "If I Can't Change Your Mind." Mould is a compelling songwriter and may be very underrated in this area. What's even more amazing is that *Copper Blue* never cracked the Billboard 200, which seems to be a crime. Sugar would manage to crack the charts with the future releases *Beaster* and *File Under Easy Listening*, but by 1995, Mould would break up the band and eventually go back to his solo career.

Sugar Red Drive – A Story Of Signs (Self Released - 2011) Hard Rock

As the music business has taken some drastic turns over time, it has been an excellent opportunity for artists to grab the bull by the horns and invest in themselves. One such band is Sugar Red Drive, whose *A Story Of Signs* is probably one album, and group that will fall off most listener's radar. *A Story Of Signs* is a very upbeat modern hard rock album. It's melodic, hard groove rock and the first three tracks alone, "Comin Down," "500 Miles" and "No Apologies" would have been hits for a band with some primary label backing. However, that is the biggest downfall of this band. Sugar Red Drive had some great management behind them and able to tour with some significant artists like Seether and Saving Able may have helped. In the end, the lack of that label support may have kept this band from other opportunities for exposure. Which honestly is a crime for a very talented group whose self-released material exceeded expectations and missed reaching more people.

Suicidal Tendencies – The Art Of Rebellion (Epic - 1992) Metal

If there was one band that was never afraid of crossing over genres, it was Suicidal Tendencies. Starting as a punk band in the early 80s, they were among the first bands to become part of the crossover thrash genre along with D.R.I. and C.O.C. They would at some point continue to change directions by adding alternative and funk metal into their heavy metal sound, with *The Art Of Rebellion* being the most experimental of the band's catalog. By 1992, vocalist Mike Muir was one of the most underrated songwriters in metal. To match that with his vocal delivery, he was in a class by himself, especially when he would go into spoken word tirades as part of the song, which really stood out. Combined with the incredible bass skills of Robert Trujillo and the dual guitar attack of Rocky George and Mike Clark, Suicidal Tendencies should have been a top tier band in the early 90s. Undoubtedly a very underappreciated band by many. You only need to give a listen to tracks like "Nobody Hears", "Monopoly Of Sorrow" and "I Wasn't Meant To Feel This/Asleep At The Wheel" to hear a band that was not afraid to follow their ideas and be one of the more original sounding hard rock/metal bands of the time. While *The Art Of Rebellion* is Suicidal Tendencies highest charting album, it should have been even bigger. Perhaps there is something in the actual name? Pretty sure having "suicidal" in your name will scare plenty of radio stations away that would have otherwise played many of the tracks on this release.

Supersuckers (photo courtesy of the band)

Supersuckers – Must've Been High (Sub Pop - 1997) Cowpunk

Since the 1980's, there have been many bands that have had a combination of country/folk into their brand of punk/alternative rock. Artists like Meat Puppets and Drivin N Cryin come to mind. In 1992, when the Supersuckers released their first album, they were high-speed punk and of course being from Seattle at the time, there was going to be some that lump them into the grunge category. Yet, there was something different about this band. They had more to bring to the table. Then in 1997, they released *Must've Been High*, which placed the band into full-on country music. There was still something punk about this release, even if it was hardly evident in the music. Standout tracks include "Roamin Around," "Hungover Together," which features Kelley Deal of The Breeders and the quick-paced country punker "Blow You Away." This is an album that will throw you off if you listen to previous Supersucker releases. Maybe that's the point. Supersuckers only prove on *Must've Been High* that a band up to a challenge can play pretty much anything. Despite not hitting a home run, it's an excellent listen.

Sweet & Lynch – Only To Rise (Frontiers - 2015) Hard Rock

Probably one of the best pairings of 80s hard rockers you will find is guitar god "Mr. Scary" George Lynch (Dokken, Lynch Mob, KXM) and one of the best vocalists of the time in Michael Sweet (Stryper, Boston). Why these two waited until 2015 to release something together is a discussion for another time, but *Only To Rise* is a significant highlight for anyone looking for that classic 80s sound. While songs like "Dying Rose" have a Dokken feel, it's just George Lynch throwing down his classic riffs. While songs like "The Wish" and "Hero-Zero" show off Sweet's incredible pipes, while many of his 80s counterparts can barely belt out their classics. This is one release that deserved a bigger audience and did not become a one-off project, as they released *Unified* in 2017.

Thin Lizzy – Renegade (Vertigo - 1981) Classic Rock

While Thin Lizzy always seems to be a band that has legions of fans, the reality is that outside of "Boys Are Back In Town," Phil Lynott and company were really nothing more than a band from Ireland that had massive success with one song. In fact, you may be hard-pressed to find people that knew any more songs outside of "Boys," "Jailbreak" and "Whiskey In The Jar," with the last song being mentioned because Metallica covered it. By 1981, Thin Lizzy was beginning to see the wheels fall off. In the early 80s, the band had obviously been influenced by some of the bands in the New Wave Of British Heavy Metal as evidenced by the sound and production. Standout tracks on *Renegade* include "The Pressure Will Blow," and "Leave This Town." However, the one song that would have fit perfectly in the bands 70s collection was "Hollywood (Down On Your Luck.)" This song displayed everything that was great about the band, just straight up rock n roll blues with high energy. Thin Lizzy would disband in its original state in 1983, with Lynott passing away in 1986. Looking over their collection, it would be a great discussion that Thin Lizzy was a very underrated band that outside of a few songs, got recognized.

Thousand Foot Krutch – Phenomenon (Tooth & Nail – 2003) Nu Metal

In Christian rock circles, Thousand Foot Krutch may be one of the biggest names in the game. In the world of nu-metal, it could be argued that they are an underrated band in the genre. The group had already been putting out releases in the mid/late 90s before their Tooth & Nail release *Phenomenon*. On this release, they put down some massive grooves, and they weave into a melodic semi-hip-hop rock sound. Even when they go into more of a rap-rock/metal direction, it still carries a melodic tone. Then in other songs, vocalist Trevor McNevan sounds eerily similar to Raine Maida of Our Lady Peace. Evidence of both sides of the band's sounds can be found on tracks like "Rawkfist," "Step To Me" and "This Is A Call." *Phenomenon* could be placed anywhere in nu-metal and various modern hard rock circles, but somewhere, this album (and its songs) did not get a lot of coverage compared to future collections from the band.

Tinted Windows – S/T (S-Curve – 2009) Power Pop

File under the "supergroup" category. When you have a combination of Cheap Trick meets Smashing Pumpkins meets Fountains of Wayne meets Hanson, this oozes power pop. This album is a sum of its parts, and if you're a fan of power pop, it's a great listen. With Taylor Hanson on vocals, the band shines, and guitarist James Iha presents a style we are not familiar with compared to his guitar work with Smashing Pumpkins. Finally, drummer Bun E. Carlos is a legend behind the kit while bassist Adam Schlesinger lays down the groove in true power pop form. Stand-out songs include the bouncy "Kind Of A Girl," the pop-punk of "Can't Get A Read On You" and the 70s boogie of "Cha Cha." It's a fun record, and while listening, you can tell these guys had a great time rocking out with each other. So why wasn't it more prominent? That's a mystery that may never be solved.

Tool – Opiate (Zoo - 1992) Alternative Metal

Tool is probably one of the most original rock bands on the planet and is never afraid to do the opposite of any trends that come and go in rock, hard rock, and metal. Many people that are into Tool may not be familiar with *Opiate*. It's a five track EP featuring some live tracks and shows that the band was more alternative metal than the progressive metal juggernaut they have become. *Opiate* was fitting for the times as the hard rock scene was changing and evolving. Along that note, Tool was a brilliant band, and *Opiate* was only a stepping stone for the group. With songs like the watch what you say anthem "Hush," the religious topics of the title track and the attitude-driven "Jerk Off," it was evident that Tool was never going to cave into trends. This album has gone platinum, and we are pretty sure that is due to fans picking up their entire collection. It is an album that does not get a lot of traction or airplay (then again, most Tool songs are too long for airplay). If you are a casual fan or it's your first time finding this band, you need to go to the beginning.

Tripping Daisy (photo courtesy of the artist)

Tripping Daisy – I Am An Elastic Firecracker (Island - 1995) Modern Rock

There are hundreds of bands from any genre and generally, have that one song everyone knows but forget about the rest of the album. One of those bands that had a clearly mistreated album are the modern rock/psychedelic sounds of Tripping Daisy. On this album, they are known for one song in "I Got A Girl." It's the 90s, and it was loud, lyrically weird and catchy. It also claimed a video spot with MTV's Beavis and Butthead at the time, so that doesn't hurt. However, there were other songs like the melodic sonic sounds of "Trip Along" and the nine-minute grunge-psych rocker "Prick" which, if made shorter could have been another radio hit for the band. This album did manage to go platinum about three years after its release. Sorry to say, Tripping Daisy didn't really put together anything that would continue to put a dent in the 90s music scene. If only people paid more attention the first time.

Triumph – Thunder Seven (MCA - 1984) Hard Rock

There have been so many great bands from Canada. Also, there have been so many bands that have lived in the shadows of other great groups. I remember reading that Theory of a Deadman was Nickelback Jr. I found that funny, then I thought Triumph at times, could have been Rush Jr. All jokes and debates aside, Triumph put out some fantastic albums in the 80s. They made a run with *Allied Forces* in 1981 and *Never Surrender* in 1983. This was the time where the band was coming into their own, and in 1984, Triumph released *Thunder Seven*. The group pulled out all the stops, and there is some tremendous musicianship throughout, and Rik Emmett's guitar work is at a different level. Some of the rocking tracks include "Spellbound," "Follow Your Heart" and "Stranger In A Strange Land." Triumph's blend of hard rock, progressive rock, and blues shows and varies track to track. However, *Thunder Seven* failed to really do anything spectacular for the band, barely making the Billboard Top 40. The next album, 1986's *A Sport Of Kings*, would give the band their first Top 40 single in "Somebody's Out There" but it was an album where the record company may have offered their input. This pretty much puts an end to

Triumph by the time the 80s would close when it should have been a continuation of the band's success.

Trivium – The Crusade (Roadrunner - 2006) Metal

While there are plenty of detractors from this band as nothing more than a Metallica copycat, Trivium has proved critics wrong again and again. Their early sound was a combination of thrash metal meets metal-core, and as they have progressed, they have become more refined. At times, develops a progressive approach to their song structure. With all that said, why *The Crusade* is not the best album in Trivium's collection is shocking. With their third album, the band pretty much abandon anything metalcore and go for more of a thrash metal approach, including ditching metal-core screams. The result is an album that is melodic, fast-paced and headbanging from top to bottom. Tracks like the fist-pumping "Anthem (We Are The Fire), "This World Can't Tear Us Apart" and "The Rising" are just a few examples of a band looking to break away from the rest of the metal pack. To add, vocalist/guitarist Matt Heafy's vocals are great and very underrated in that respect. Meanwhile, the two-guitar attack of Corey Beaulieu and Heafy are among the best duos in hard rock/metal. With all that said, this album only managed a Top 25 spot on the charts and the band would go back to some of their metal-core roots with Shogun in 2008. Over the years, the group has come back to more of what they did with *The Crusade* in their follow-up releases, 2013's *Vengeance Falls*, 2015's *Silence In The Snow* and 2017's *The Sin And The Sentence*, only enhancing their musical catalog.

Twisted Sister – Under The Blade (Secret - 1982) Hard Rock

The roots of Twisted Sister date all the way back to 1972 and after rolling through the New York rock scene, Dee Snider and company release Under the Blade ten years later. Twisted Sister can be described in two ways. First, they can be a very aggressive hard rock band that is full of power and angst. Then, they have this 70s glam rock style like the New York Dolls, full of energy and melody. Add some crazy outfits, all the makeup that Kiss did not use in their kit and you have every mother's nightmare, Twisted Sister. *Under The Blade* is two albums before the hugely successful *Stay Hungry* album, but this album has all the same elements. Standout tracks include "I'll Never Grow Up," "Shoot Em Down" and "What You Don't Know" giving you a taste of what this album represents. This may be more of an underground album for most unless you are a diehard fan, but it's the stepping stone for the band's first major label release *You Can't Stop Rock N Roll*. While they sometimes get more noticed for their look and hooky songs, Twisted Sister proves early on that they are more than a one trick pony and *Under The Blade* clearly sets that tone.

Type O Negative – World Coming Down (Roadrunner - 1999) Metal

Another band that could be considered in the underappreciated category. Some groups can be put in a class by themselves just based on that they sound like nobody else. A true original artist. That was Type O Negative, a band that took elements of goth rock and metal, making it unique, compelling, spooky, and embracing. Add the lyrical stylings of Peter Steele's humor into the mix, and you have a band that may never be duplicated. The early 90s gives the group some success, and as the decade closed, Type O Negative was heading back to more of a cult status. In fact, they probably liked it that way. In 1999, they would release *World Coming Down* and could very well be their most overlooked album. The dark vocals of Steele combined with the Sabbath driven tone of the music, the eerie synthesizers, and songs clocking in on average of over 6 minutes per track. They have a creation ready for headphones. Significant tracks include "Everyone I Love Is Dead" and "Everything Dies." Another great track "All Hallows Eve" is the perfect song for your Halloween party or a trip to your local cemetery.

The band even makes The Beatles "Day Tripper" creepy, and that's a compliment. *World Coming Down* is as good as *Bloody Kisses* and *October Rust* before it and should be in the conversation with those classics.

U-Z

Jim Santora with Klaus Eichstadt of Ugly Kid Joe (photo by Ed Mason)

Ugly Kid Joe – Motel California (Castle - 1996) Hard Rock

If we were filing artists based on why their success (or non-success) happened, for Ugly Kid Joe, the answer would be miscategorized. UKJ was a hard rock band that was more of a metal/funk hybrid than glam metal. Take elements of Judas Priest and Red Hot Chili Peppers, and you just get a taste of what their sound was like. In the early 90s, they scored a massive hit with the power ballad cover of "Cat's in The Cradle." By the time 1995 rolled in and they released the heavy/funky/industrial style Menace to Sobriety, it was almost ignored. In 1996, UKJ put out *Motel California,* an album where the band placed all their influences onto the floor and crushed it. The album displays a musical hodgepodge of classic hard rock, metal, punk, and funk. Featuring a two-guitar attack and the excellent vocal stylings of Whitfield Crane, every song stands out just from the diverse musical arrangements. Among all the great songs on this recording, the melodic, classic rock of "Would You Like To Be There," the hard rock driving "Dialogue" and the southern rock inspired "Undertow" are the standouts. Ugly Kid Joe should have been more classified with late 80s/90s bands that were a heavier alternative rock than the tail end of 80s glam metal. Perhaps that would have kept albums like *Motel California* from being an afterthought for most.

Utah Saints – S/T (London - 1991) Electronica

As the 80s was winding down and the 90s were approaching, there was plenty of shifts in rock genres. Also, in the mix was electronica, which many new wave bands infused into their sounds. In the 1990's, electronica had started to become a thing where DJ's were the musicians. Before Moby, Fatboy Slim, Chemical Brothers, and the Crystal Method, there was Utah Saints, a duo out of London who crafted electronic music with rock. They were exceptional and captured fans in the alternative/modern rock world, but their debut was not a massive success. What they did have were structured tracks that caught ears with their danceable grooves and for additional components that made their songs have some rock edge to them. Maybe the objective was to be plenty of dance for the club and enough rock for the alternative rock club (yes, there was a time where that was a thing)? They did score a Top 100 song from "Something Good" which featured a Kate Bush sample from her song "Cloudbursting." Other standout tracks include "What Can You Do For Me," featuring samples from Eurythmics, Gwen Guthrie, and Kiss, and "I Want You" contains a sample of Slayer's "War Ensemble" as part of the primary structure of the track. This was one album, if not famous, was something different and apparently was an influence on upcoming artists in the 90s that approached a rock influence in their electronic music direction.

Van Stephenson – Righteous Anger (MCA - 1984) Rock

While the 1980's had a certain gloss that the rock bands of the 70s did not have, it made plenty of groups available thanks to MTV becoming the forefront of music being visual, as well as audio. Of course, there were plenty of artists trying to take their cut and solo artist Van Stephenson was in the mix. Most people that remember Van Stephenson might have thought it was the name of the band. As it turns out, he was a solo artist, and in 1984, would release his second album *Righteous Anger.* This album is led by the Top 40 hit, "Modern Day Delilah," which should have been an even bigger hit. Other songs like "What the Big Girls Do" and the ballad "Others Only Dream" was well-crafted songs full of big guitars, keyboards, and solid vocals. Van Stephenson, however, could be compared to Bryan Adams and Don Henley during the time, which probably answers the question as to why he was not a bigger name. Success would find Stephenson in the 90s when he became the lead guitarist for country band Blackhawk. Sadly, Stephenson passed away in 2001.

War Babies – S/T (Columbia - 1991) Hard Rock

In the 1980's, TKO vocalist Brad Sinsel was one of the more under the radar bands on the Sunset Strip. They had one song "I Wanna Fight" that received some minor traction, but nothing that really materialized into top-tier status. Fast forward years later and Brad's next effort War Babies was coming in at the right time of the grunge explosion. The LA band made their way to Seattle and rubbed shoulders with Mother Love Bone, Soundgarden, and Alice In Chains and managed to secure a record deal with

Columbia in the process. On this self-titled record, it's sort of a grunge/hair band mashup. Vocally, Sinsel shows off a lot of emotion, and you can hear the stylings that made grunge music a thing in the early 90s. Songs like "Cry Yourself To Sleep," "Hang Me Up" and "Sea Of Madness" set the tone of an excellent sounding record. What's unfortunate is that they were a band that was one and done. Apparently, they still sounded too much like all the glam metal bands and got pushed aside. Maybe War Babies needed to be a little more aggressive or abrasive? Perhaps they need to drop tune those guitars a little more? Whatever it was, there is no mistaking that War Babies had a great sound and were just caught at a genre crossroads.

Waterdown (photo courtesy of the artist)

Waterdown – All Riot (Victory - 2006) Hardcore

Direct from Germany come Waterdown, who in 2006 released their third album on hardcore/punk label Victory Records. This was one band that had a great combination of aggressive and melodic vocals to go along with a heavy punk/metal sound. Songs like "Cut The Cord," "My Hopelessness In Me" and "Chewing On Lies" are just a sampling of the mosh pit frenzy this band laid down. The problem with *All Riot* is that they may have been in the mix at the wrong time for the label. By 2006, Victory was laying all their chips on bands like Hawthorne Heights, Atreyu and Taking Back Sunday. So perhaps Waterdown was just left on their own with hopes fans of other bands from the roster would take notice. Sadly, they didn't and missed a great album. Waterdown would eventually be off the label and have been defunct since 2012.

Weaving The Fate (photo courtesy of the artist)

Weaving The Fate – WTF The EP (Universal - 2012) Nu Metal

Weaving the Fate is a band that was still carrying the nu-metal torch in 2012. The group used a combination of metal and rap/hip-hop stylings. They had a sound that was infectious and made some noise with songs like the mosh hop grooves of "Rack City." WTF brings the party with another standout track like the nu-metal style of "Str8 To The Bottom", which combines so many influences in rock, metal, rap/hip-hop and funk it's hard to really classify. Then they bring hard rock and funk stylings into "The Fall." Every song you think you have WTF figured out, they do something different and refreshing. The big problem with this album is that it's only an EP. Just five excellent tracks to enjoy. Sadly, not much from WTF since, which is a shame because they were a band that had an exciting sound and really knew how to lay down a groove.

Weezer – Pinkerton (DGC - 1996) Alternative Rock

Probably one of the more significant "cult" albums you will find in these pages. Weezer is one of the premier bands in Alternative Rock based on longevity, success, and influence amongst other bands. In 1994, they would release the *Blue Album* which today remains as one of the best rock albums that people must listen to (but we will discuss that in another book). When it was time for a follow-up, the band would release *Pinkerton* in 1996. The album was self-produced by the band and much darker than their debut. It's really a gutsy move considering the band could have continued following the path they already laid out. Songs like "Tired Of Sex," "El Scorcho" and "Pink Triangle" still showed what the Weezer formula. The combination of fuzzed-out power pop with creative, sometimes odd and humorous lyrics. Vocalist/guitarist and primary songwriter Rivers Cuomo is a lyrical genius who can find ways on *Pinkerton* to place Public Enemy, Green Day and ECW wrestlers into a song and make it work (El Scorcho). Fair weather fans of the band did not get what Weezer was doing, so they passed up on *Pinkerton*. The group would not release another album until the hugely successful *Green Album* in 2001. As the years have gone by, *Pinkerton* has slowly been re-captured by new fans, and old fans are trying to re-embrace the album. It's a classic album and is as good as anything else in the band's collection.

White Witch – A Spiritual Greeting (Capricorn - 1974)   Psychedelic Rock

A band that was dubbed the Black Sabbath of the South? While anything or anyone being compared to Black Sabbath could be a good thing, it really doesn't tell the whole story of White Witch. With *A Spiritual Greeting*, the band's 2nd album, they covered psychedelic rock, southern boogie, progressive rock and at times pop rock. White Witch was also labeled as a glam rock band, but somehow that doesn't quite fit what the group was doing. Tracks that deserve a much overdue listen include "Slick Witch," "We'll All Ride High (Money Bags)" and are they predicting the future with "Class of 2000"? *A Spiritual Greeting* is a unique listen, and if you are a fan of early psychedelic and prog rock, this might be an overlooked band that needs to be in your collection. One had to wonder what was in the water (or the drugs) when White Witch put together their blend of rock back in the early 70s.

Winger – Pull (Atlantic - 1993) Hard Rock

Here is one band that has been the "Butthead" of jokes pretty much for the rest of their lives. Winger came out of the late 80's, and even though they were classified with the hair bands, they were really so much more. They had a progressive rock style to their sound, so musically, Winger had a wider range. After the first two albums go platinum, then comes MTV's *Beavis and Butthead* and they eventually make fun of the video for "Seventeen." Then the neighbor Stewart wears a Winger shirt to their AC/DC, and Metallica shirts and all the sudden, Winger is the worst band on the planet. That is not fair to this talented group. You could have picked any other lame band of that time, and they chose Kip and the boys. So, let's get to *Pull*, which is by far the best example of the band moving in more of a progressive direction. The melodies are still there, and Kip Winger is a vastly underrated vocalist. Add the amazing guitar work of Reb Beach and the drum work of Rod Morgenstein, and this is an album that pretty much got forgotten. This was also an album done as a trio as keyboardist Paul Taylor had left the band, which did not have any effects on the overall production of this album. Standout tracks include "In My Veins," "Down Incognito" and "In For The Kill." This album should have been one that stood out above the grunge movement of the 90s. Now that those two knuckleheads are off the air, it's ok to give *Pull* a listen as soon as possible.

Zebra – No Tellin' Lies (Atlantic- 1984) Hard Rock

After the success of Zebra's debut in 1983, what could this trio come up with next? Eighteen months later, they would follow up with *No Tellin' Lies*, which if you look at pure numbers was considered a commercial failure. Those naysayers need to take another listen to Randy Jackson and company deliver nothing but great rock throughout. A dash of Led Zeppelin meets ELP meets Louisiana/NYC hybrid that makes Zebra unique, to begin with. "Bears" is the classic track from this release, focusing more on keyboards but showcase both Jackson's falsetto and lead guitar solo. Other tracks like the hard rocker "Wait Until The Summers Gone," the prog stylings of "But No More" and the softer ballad "Lullaby" just further showcase a band that can be more than three chords and a high-pitched singer. Also, to note, Felix Hanneman shows his underrated skills on the bass through all ten tracks.

Zodiac Mindwarp and the Love Reaction – Tattooed Beat Messiah (Mercury - 1988) Hard Rock

The late 80s were a strange trip to rock. The musical landscape changed and you could sense it. Hard rock, metal, and alternative rock were all starting to gain some steam and change direction heading into the 90s. Some of the bands trying to make some noise were Zodiac Mindwarp, whose *Tattooed Beat Messiah* took everything you knew about 80s rock and smacked you in the face. The album oozed with excess and was a sex-filled emotional thrill ride. Standout tracks include "Prime Mover," "Backseat Education" and "Skull Spark Joker" are just starters for the mayhem this album puts you in. They had some success in the UK, but in the US, they were popular amongst the college radio stations, and that's where it ends. There are plenty of people that turned their nose up at Zodiac Mindwarp as nothing more than a gimmick. Regardless of that opinion, this was one album that does not disappoint.

Underrated Rock Lists

After spending over two years researching and writing this book, I thought it would be fun to gather up some lists. An entertaining guide and observations I came up with while documenting, critiquing and just anything else that would pop up in my head. Again, like in our introduction: Will you disagree? I have no doubt you will, and this will only continue the discussions of this book. Enjoy!

The 15 Albums In The Underrated Rock Book You Need To Hear:
Cheap Trick – *All Shook Up*
Our Lady Peace – *Spiritual Machines*
Aerosmith – *Night In The Ruts*
7 Seconds – *The Music The Message*
Corrosion Of Conformity – *America's Volume Dealer*
Game Theory – *Lolita Nation*
Dinosaur jr – *Your Living All Over Me*
Drivin N Cryin – *Whisper Tames The Lion*
Electric Light Orchestra – *On The Third Day*
King's X – *Ear Candy*
Suicidal Tendencies – *The Art Of Rebellion*
The Cars – *Panorama*
Ned's Atomic Dustbin – *God Fodder*
The Nils – *The Nils*
Kansas - *Masque*

This list is in no particular order, but if there are 15 albums to start with and listen to from front to back, these are the essentials from the URB…

Ten Bands That Author Became A Fan Of While Writing The Book:

- Dread Zeppelin
- Heaven & Earth
- Information Society
- Legs Diamond
- Mother's Finest
- Nashville Pussy
- Operator
- Robert Bradley's Blackwater Surprise
- The High Speed Scene
- The Mars Volta

If some of these bands you are already fans of. Then you are well ahead of the game than I was. I will never know why I passed these artists by, but my research into the book re-introduced me to some great music and some very overlooked albums as well.

The Top 5 Most Underrated Songwriters In URB:

1. Kevn Kinney (Drivin N Cryin)
2. Pat DiNizio (The Smithereens)
3. Scott Miller (Game Theory/Loud Family)
4. Sean Danielsen (Smile Empty Soul)
5. Mike Muir (Suicidal Tendencies)

These five songwriters have a real gift. Some are great storytellers, while others make you think and feel. When you get a moment, one album does not do these writers justice. Take the time to listen to their discography's in detail.

The Most Underrated and Overlooked Artists Of All Time:

This list is based on bands that make our albums list. Many of these bands have plenty of albums in their discography that needs to be revisited as soon as possible.

1) **King's X** – Hardcore following going on 30+ years. Some great albums, tours with awesome bands and even a Woodstock performance couldn't get this trio to take off.

2) **Drivin N Cryin** – A band that could play hard rock, punk, folk, and country and sometimes all on the same album. A very diverse group musically that had a chance at success, and then it was gone. Another group with 30+ years together.

3) **Game Theory/Loud Family** – Both bands are led by the late Scott Miller, which is why they are mentioned together. Miller was a musical genius that most people didn't get. A recent album of unfinished work was recently created as a Game Theory album with help from Peter Buck (R.E.M.) among others.

4) **The Dandy Warhols** – A band that is huge around the world and not nearly as popular as they should be in the US. They may very well be the best alternative/modern rock band to come out of the 1990's that most people cast off. Still releasing albums and touring today.

5) **Raging Slab** – A band that can be classified as hard rock, southern rock, and stoner rock. They always sounded like a fun band to hang around and drink with. Plenty of southern boogie and slide guitars to go around. The group got lumped into glam metal at the end of the 80s, survived and got into the alternative 90's with not much more than a core audience. One of the most under the radar bands of their genre.

6) **Jeffrey Gaines** – Known more for his version of Peter Gabriel's "In Your Eyes" than the rest of his collection. Gaines continues to release albums and tour and is an excellent live performer. When the 90s had plenty of acoustic performers getting the spotlight, Gaines was not on that stage, yet there are plenty of songs in his catalog that would say otherwise.

7) **Danko Jones** – This Canadian Trio is known worldwide, and despite some minor spins over the last 10 years, they are not very respected in the US. If you want straight up power rock, you don't have to look too far to check out one fantastic group. Another band still putting out albums and cranking for whoever will listen.

8) **Zebra** – A band that started in the 1970's but did not get their big break until the early 80s. This trio had a combination of Prog Rock meets Led Zeppelin which caught attention early on. However, their music seemed to get deeply rooted in other hard rock and metal of the time, and by the time the 90s rolled along, Zebra was an afterthought. The band has reunited in the last 10-15+ years to continue to perform for audiences.

9) **Smile Empty Soul** – A band from the early 2000's whose first six albums were on six different labels. That should tell you something about them. Very talented hard rock three piece with lyrics that displayed the angst of youth. Despite the band's best efforts, they never became a top-tier band in the post-grunge/alternative metal genres. Still releasing albums and touring today.

10) **The Forecast** – A midwestern band that combined emo rock with indie rock and country. This band was something special to listen to, and they come onto the scene at a time where melodic hardcore and screamo bands were moving up the ranks. While the group was rubbing shoulders with the likes of Hawthorne Heights and others, they were just different enough to have a dedicated following but not one that would make them a household name.

Bands/Artists In The Underrated Rock Book That Are Members Of The Rock N Roll Hall Of Fame:

- AC/DC
- Aerosmith
- Beastie Boys
- The Cars
- Cheap Trick
- Christine McVie (Fleetwood Mac)
- Dire Straits
- Electric Light Orchestra
- Joan Jett
- Kiss
- Led Zeppelin
- Neil Young
- R.E.M.
- Red Hot Chili Peppers
- Run DMC
- Rush

For every band that has entered the Hall of Fame, there is that one album that gets overlooked. Most of these bands have longevity and substantial discography. If you are not a fan of these artists, hopefully listening to their selected album for the Underrated Rock Book will be a good starting point and lead you to additional music from some greats.

Artists That Appear In The Underrated Rock Book Twice (or more): (Not a complete list as we are sure we missed someone)

- Greg Hetson – Guitarist on Bad Religion (The Grey Race) and Circle Jerks (VI)
- Roman Glick – Bass on Brother Cane (Self Titled) and Jackyl (Best In Show)
- George Lynch – Guitarist on Dokken (Dysfunctional) and Sweet & Lynch (Only To Rise)
- Bev Bevan – Drummer on Electric Light Orchestra (On The Third Day) and The Move (Shazam)
- Drivin N Cryin/Kevn Kinney on Drivin N Cryin (Whisper Tames The Lion) and Kevn Kinney (Macdougal Blues)
- Dug Pinnick – Vocalist/Bassist on King's X (Ear Candy) and Poundhound (Massive Grooves)
- "Fast" Eddie Clarke -Guitarist on Motorhead (Self-Titled) and Fastway (Self-Titled)
- Ric Ocasek – Vocalist/Guitarist/Producer on The Cars (Panorama), Rick Ocasek (Beatitude) and Bad Religion (The Grey Race)
- Sebastian Bach – Vocalist on solo release (Kicking and Screaming) and Skid Row (Subhuman Race)
- James Iha – Guitarist on Smashing Pumpkins (Gish) and Tinted Windows (Self-Titled)
- Bun E. Carlos – Drummer on Cheap Trick (All Shook Up) and Tinted Windows (Self-Titled)
- Scott Miller – Vocalist/Guitarist on Game Theory (Lolita Nation) and The Loud Family (Interbabe Concern)
- Mark Mendoza – Bassist on The Dictators (Manifest Destiny) and Twisted Sister (Under The Blade)

- Jack Irons – Drummer on Red Hot Chili Peppers (The Uplift Mofo Party Plan) and Neil Young (Mirror Ball)
- Chris Goss – Guitarist, Vocalist and Producer on Masters Of Reality (S/T) and Kyuss (And The Circus Leaves Town)
- Flea – Bass on Red Hot Chili Peppers (Uplift Mofo Party Plan) and The Mars Volta (De-Loused In The Comatorium)
- Juliana Hatfield – Vocals, Guitars on solo release (Only Everything) and backing Vocals on The Lemonheads (Come On Feel The Lemonheads)
- Raine Maida – Vocals on Our Lady Peace (Spiritual Machines) and Songwriter on Kelly Clarkson (My December)
- Peter Buck – Guitarist on R.E.M. (Monster) and Guitarist, Producer on Kevn Kinney (Macdougal Blues)
- Bob Mould – Vocal, Guitars on Sugar (Copper Blue) and producer on Magnapop (Hot Boxing)

Artists That Were Considered For The Underrated Rock Book :
Alice Cooper, Quiet Riot, Andy Taylor (Duran Duran), Ramones, The Who, Paul McCartney, Pink Floyd, Def Leppard, Metallica, Vanilla Fudge, The Offspring, Black Sabbath, Yes, Sweet, Warrant, White Lion, Taproot, Montrose, Britney Fox, Fates Warning, Kix, Helix, John Lennon, Testament, Emerson, Lake & Palmer, Poison, Overkill, Dag Nasty, Pearl Jam, UFO, Van Halen, Sammy Hagar, Sanctuary, Saga, Framing Hanley, Sepultura, Faster Pussycat, Best Coast, Hawkwind, Robin Zander, Stryper, The National, RTZ, Blackfoot, 32 Leaves, Crossfade, U.P.O., Annihilator, Faith Or Fear, Kim Mitchell, GWAR, Focus, Keel, Lucifer's Friend, Elvis Costello, Cornershop, Marcy Playground, Y&T, Asia, Rains, Collective Soul, Black Crowes, James Young (Styx), Mott The Hoople, Neverland, Lindsey Buckingham, Monsterworks, Great White, Hurricane, Public Image Limited, Bloodhound Gang, Grip Inc., Dead Milkmen, Gruntruck, Foghat, Symphony X, Ozzy Osbourne, Dio, Iron Maiden, The Fashion, Miss Crazy, Fools For Rowan, Leatherwolf, Fifth Angel Exhorder, God Is LSD, Sloan, Flipp, The Almost, Widowmaker, Urge Overkill to name a few of the artists that didn't make the cut… Maybe a Volume 2?

The Ultimate Underrated Rock Playlist !!!
200 Songs – 200 Artists!   Enjoy!

7 Seconds – See You Tomorrow

54.40 – Walk In Line

77 – Down And Dirty

1978 Champs – Alamo

AC/DC – Shake Your Foundations

Aerosmith – Three Mile Smile

Alice In Chains – Brother

The Angels – Dogs Are Talking

Ancient VVisdom – Chaos Will Reign

And You Will Know Us By The Trail Of Dead – A Classic Art Showcase

Angel – Tower

Anthrax – Fueled

April Wine – I Like To Rock

The Atomic Bitchwax – The Destroyer

Audiovent – The Energy

The Bags – Spread It Around

Bad Brains - Soul Craft

Bad Religion – A Walk

Badlands – Winter's Call

Baalam and the Angel – I'll Show You Something Special

Beastie Boys – Jimmy James

Billy Squier – Don't Let Me Go

Blue Oyster Cult – Take Me Away

Blues Traveler – Carolina Blues

Boston – Cool The Engines

Brother Cane – Got No Shame

The Cars – Don't Tell Me No

Cats In Boots – Shotgun Sally

Cheap Trick – Stop This Game

Child's Play – My Bottle

Christine McVie – Got A Hold On Me

Circle Jerks – Status Clinger

Circus Of Power – Last Call Rosie

City Boy – Oddball Dance

Clutch – The Soapmakers

Concrete Blonde – Still In Hollywood

Core – Hate Me Harder

Corrosion Of Conformity – Stare Too Long

Crimson Glory – Painted Skies

The Cult – War (The Process)

D.A.D. – Sleeping My Day Away

The Dandy Warhols – Minnesoter

Danko Jones – Take Me Home

Dead Boys – 3rd Generation Nation

Detective – Competition

Deuce – I Came To Party

Devo – Later Is Now

The Dictators – Sleepin With The TV On

Dinosaur jr – Sludgefeast

Dire Straits – Industrial Disease

Dirty Looks – L.A. Anna

Dokken – Too High To Fly

Downset – Empower

Dread Zeppelin – Heartbreaker /Heartbreak Hotel

Drivin N Cryin – Check Your Tears At The Door

Duran Duran – All She Wants Is

Earshot – Misunderstood

Eclipse – Wake Me Up

Electric Light Orchestra – Ma-Ma-Ma-Belle

Elf – Hoochie Coochie Lady

Fair To Midland – Tall Tales Sound Like Sour Grapes

Fastway – Heft

Firehose – For The Singer Of R.E.M.

Flyleaf – Marionette

The Forecast – A Fistfight For Our Fathers

Fu Manchu – Over The Edge

Game Theory – Nothing New

The Godfathers – Cause I Said So

The Godz – Gotta Keep A Runnin

Goo Goo Dolls – Up Yours

Gothic Slam – Who Died And Made Your God

Harvey Danger – Sad Sweetheart Of The Rodeo

Hawthorne Heights – Taken By The Dark

Heaven & Earth – No Money No Love

Helmet – Milquetoast

The High Speed Scene – The I-Roc Song

HSAS – Top Of The Rock

I, Omega – Half Way Home

Icarus Witch – (We Are) The New Revolution

Incubus – New Skin

Information Society – On The Outside

INXS – Make Your Peace

Jackyl – Encore

Jeffrey Gaines – Hero In Me

Judas Priest – Victim Of Changes

Juliana Hatfield – Universal Heartbeat

Kansas – Icarus (Borne On Wings Of Steel)

Kelly Clarkson – Never Again

Kevn Kinney – Gotta Get Outta Here

Killer Dwarfs – Comin Through

King's X – Mississippi Moon

Kiss – The Oath

The Knack – River Of Sighs

Kopek – Love Is Dead

Kyuss – One Inch Man

L7 – Can I Run

The Leaving Trains – Walking With You

Led Zeppelin – Nobody's Fault But Mine

Legs Diamond – A Diamond Is A Hard Rock

The Lemonheads – Into Your Arms

Life Of Agony – Love To Let You Down

Lillian Axe – Caged In

Living Colour – Leave It Alone

Lizzy Borden – Me Against The World

Local H – Cook Magnet

The Loud Family – Don't Respond She Can Tell

Loudness – Crazy Nights

Love/Hate – Blackout In The Red Room

Magnapop – Here It Comes

Mama's Boys – Needle In The Groove

The Mars Volta – Drunkship Of Lanterns

Marty Casey and Lovehammers – Casualty

Mass – Do You Love Me

Masters Of Reality – John Brown

Matthew Sweet – Dinosaur Act

Medieval – Blood And Anger

Megadeth – Train Of Consequences

Method Of Destruction – Get A Real Job

Ministry – Cannibal Song

Mos Generator – Lonely One Kenobi

Mother's Finest – Movin On

Motley Crue – Misunderstood

Motorhead – Vibrator

The Move – Don't Make My Baby Blue

Naked Raygun – Soldiers Requiem

Nashville Pussy – Shoot First And Run Like Hell

Neds Atomic Dustbin – Throwing Things

Neil Young – Downtown

New England – Don't Ever Want To Lose Ya

Nickelback – Old Enough

The Nils – Wicked Politician

Nothing More – Fat Kid

Operator – Soulcrusher

Orgy – Fiction (Dreams In Digital)

Our Lady Peace – Everyone's A Junkie

Pallbearer – World's Apart

Papa Roach – M-80 (Explosive Energy Movement)

Pete Shelley – Telephone Operator

Poundhound – Soul

Pray For The Soul Of Betty – Drift

The Presidents Of The United States Of America – Tiki God

Puya – Fundamental

Queensryche – Hundred Mile Stare

R.E.M. – Strange Currencies

Raging Slab – Geronimo

Ratt – Over The Edge

Recovery Council – Wool

The Red Hot Chili Peppers – Organic Anti Beat Box Band

Redlight King – Born To Rise

Red Light Chemistry – Paralyzed

Red Rider – Human Race

Reo Speedwagon – The Key

Ric Ocasek – Something To Grab For

Robert Bradley's Blackwater Surprise – Once Upon A Time

The Runaways – Fantasies

Run DMC – Rock Show

Rush – Between The Wheels

Saliva – Two Steps Back

Sebastian Bach – Tunnelvision

Seven Circle Sunrise – After All

Shaman's Harvest – Country As F***

Shooting Star – Hang On For Your Life

Shotgun Messiah – I'm A Gun

Skid Row – Beat Yourself Blind

Slade – Gudbuy T'Jane

Smash Into Pieces – Disaster Highway

The Smashing Pumpkins – Rhinoceros

Smile Empty Soul – Here's To Another

The Smithereens – Drown In My Own Tears

Soul Asylum – Cartoon

Sound Barrier – Rock Without The Roll

Soundgarden – Big Dumb Sex

Squirrel Bait – Sun God

Starz – Sing It Shout It

Styx – Why Me

Sugar – Changes

Sugar Red Drive – 500 Miles

Suicidal Tendencies – I Wasn't Meant To Feel This/Asleep At The Wheel

Supersuckers – Roamin Around

Sweet & Lynch – Dying Rose

Thin Lizzy – Hollywood (Down On Your Luck)

Thousand Foot Krutch – This Is A Call

Tinted Windows – Kind Of A Girl
Tool – Jerk Off
Tripping Daisy – I Got A Girl
Triumph – Follow Your Heart
Trivium – This World Can't Tear Us Apart
Twisted Sister – Shoot Em Down
Type O Negative – Everyone I Love Is Dead
Ugly Kid Joe – Would You Like To Be There
Utah Saints – Something Good
Van Stephenson – Modern Day Delilah
War Babies – Cry Yourself To Sleep
Waterdown – My Hopelessness In Me
Weaving The Fate – Rack City
Weezer – El Scorcho
White Witch – Slick Witch
Winger – In My Veins
Zebra – Bears
Zodiac Mindwarp And The Love Reaction – Backseat Education

About the Author

Jim Santora Jr's first published piece was with the Hammonton News, a local town newspaper in Hammonton NJ, where he grew up. He was working as a sports writer for the paper in 1988 while going to college. His first passion was radio, where he would be on the air at WACC Campus Radio (Atlantic Community College), where he also served as music director and general manager. He would also spend summers as a DJ at WLFR (Stockton College). All of this took place between 1987-1990.

He would go on to form Rock N Roll Express Entertainment and was a DJ and Karaoke host for a good portion of the 1990's. He continued his writing, working as a beat reporter for the Beachcomber, located in Margate, NJ. He also became a music review critic, writing for In Tune Magazine, located in the Atlantic City NJ area. During this time, he would become a feature writer, covering live events and interviews. Some pieces of his work included coverage of Tom Petty, Deftones, Ugly Kid Joe, Type O Negative and Drivin N Cryin. It was also in the early 90s that he would be in the band Hideous Heinous. A collection of the band's music went to Spin Magazine as part of their "Worst Band in America" contest. The group would not win, but the music must have been good (or bad) enough to be mentioned in an article by the magazine as well as a feature shown on CNN.

Heading into the late 90s to early 2000's, he would have a radio show on WNJC, located in Washington Twp. NJ. This show would eventually become the first of his internet programs, airing on Live365. His passion for internet radio programs would continue in the late 2000's until 2015, hosting "The Jim Santora Show" on Hot Rocks Radio, Blog Talk Radio and eventually his own radio station, SH ROCK. The program was successful and some of the interviews that the program had included members of Asking Alexandria, Saliva, Dokken, King's X, The Dandy Warhols, Zebra, The Outlaws, Kansas, L.A. Guns, Stryper, Smile Empty Soul, and Great White among others.

From 2005-2011, Jim was the lead vocalist of the bands 77LeSabre and Redliner. With 77LeSabre, he would release "Ride" in 2006. In 2009 with Redliner, "Vengeance" was released. Both groups performed all over New Jersey, Pennsylvania, Delaware, and Maryland and shared the stage with Tesla, Epica, Voodoo Blue, and Threat Signal. He also was involved in various show production during this time, working with multiple artists including Chris Barron of Spin Doctors, Omnisoul and Suicide City.

Jim is married to his wife, Jennifer and has two children, Joshua, and Abbie.

Links

Below are some links to check out from some of our friends that helped support the creation of this book:

- Philly Rock Radio – www.phillyrockradio.com
- The Saloon - www.phillyrockradio.com/the-saloon-rock-club
- Musical WTH - www.facebook.com/MusicalWTH/

To find out more on Underrated Rock Book:

www.underratedrockbook.com

Feel free to send us feedback:
contact@underratedrockbook.com
Tell us what you thought of the book.
Let us know which albums you agree or disagree with.
Also, feel free to give us suggestions!

Join us on Social Media:

Facebook - @underratedrockbook
Twitter - @URockBook

90376192R00099

Made in the USA
Middletown, DE
22 September 2018